Other

WESLEYAN POETRY

OTHER

British and Irish Poetry since 1970

Richard Caddel and Peter Quartermain, editors

Wesleyan University Press

Published by University Press of New England

Hanover and London

Wesleyan University Press

Published by University Press of New England, Hanover, NH 03755

This collection © 1999 by Wesleyan University

Introduction © 1999 by Richard Caddel and Peter Quartermain

Printed in the United States of America   5 4 3 2 1

CIP data appear at the end of the book

Cover art: Antony Gormley, *Field for the British Isles*, copyright © 1993 by the artist

The editors gratefully acknowledge the following for permission to reprint material to which they hold copyright:

John Agard, whose poems are reprinted herein by kind permission of John Agard c/o Caroline Sheldon Literary Agency: "Half-caste" from *Get Back, Pimple*, published by Viking 1996; "Palm Tree King," "Listen Mr Oxford Don" from *Mangoes & Bullets*, published by the Bodley Head 1993.

Tony Baker for poems from *Scrins* (Pig Press 1989) and uncollected work.

Anthony Barnett for poems from *Carp and Rubato* (Invisible Books 1995). Copyright © 1995 Anthony Barnett.

Richard Caddel for poems from *Uncertain Time* (Galloping Dog 1990) and *Larksong Signal* (Shearsman 1997).

Jacket web magazine for an earlier version of *A Fair Field Full of Folk* by Richard Caddel and Peter Quartermain.

Cris Cheek for work from *Fogs* (uncollected).

Thomas A Clark for poems from *Sixteen Sonnets* (Moschatel Press 1981), *Out of The Wind* (Moschatel Press 1984), and unpublished work.

Bob Cobbing for work from *Beethoven Today* (Writers Forum 1970), *Sonic Icons* (Writers Forum 1970), *Processual Four* (Writers Forum 1983), *Prosexual* (Writers Forum 1984), and *Gibbering His Wares (Collected Poems v. 15)* (Object Permanence 1996).

The Estate of Brian Coffey for work corrected from *Poems and Versions* (Dedalus Press 1991).

Kelvin Corcoran for work from *Lyric Lyric* (Reality Street 1993) and *Melanie's Book* (West House 1996).

Andrew Crozier for work from *All Where Each Is* (Allardyce, Barnett 1985) and *Ghosts in the Corridor* (Paladin, 1992).

Fred D'Aguiar for poems from *Mama Dot* (Chatto 1985), *Airy Hall* (Chatto 1989), *British Subjects* (Bloodaxe 1993), and uncollected work.

Ken Edwards for poems from *Intensive Care* (Pig Press 1986), *Good Science* (Roof Books 1992), and *3600 Weekends* (Oasis 1993).

Peter Finch for work from *Selected Poems* (Poetry Wales 1987) and *Antibodies* (Stride 1997).

Allen Fisher for work from *Brixton Fractals* (Aloes Books 1985), *Stepping Out* (Pig Press 1989), and uncollected work.

(Acknowledgments continued on p. 279)

To Ann Caddel and Meredith Quartermain

and in memory of

Tom Caddel (1976–1995)

Contents

Introduction—A Fair Field Full of Folk

The British Isles have long been, self-evidently, crowded, complex, and packed with chaotic overlays of cultures—local, imported, or created—which develop and intermix constantly. Langland's fourteenth-century field of folk was already an intensely plural society, where elements of Saxon, Norman, and Cymric were evident alongside each other, with strong elements of latinate church culture, and, never far away, mainland European culture jostling alongside the other elements of linguistic mix. Diverse cultures sometimes conflict violently, or sometimes make uneasy alliances, and sometimes, perhaps by chance, give rise to the creation of new forms or achievements. About the only thing that is not possible in such a pluralistic, fragmenting, evolving society is a unitary, closed-system approach to culture, an insistence on a single "great tradition" that can justify any degree of cultural domination. And yet at present the organs of this culture—from opera and literature to government—remain unshakably monolithic and centralised: to look at the central products of this culture is to be reminded just how assertive the "mainstream" has been, and how marginalised its alternatives have seemed at times.

It is not the function of this introduction to describe in detail the development of this "mainstream," nor is it our intention to dismiss it as devoid of worth. However, it is necessary to suggest why it has appeared such an alienating experience for so many of the writers here, and why, finally, most of them reject it: "mainstream" in this context may be said to include the narrow lineage of contemporary poets from Philip Larkin to Craig Raine and Simon Armitage, and encompassing their attendant "collectives" (Movement, Martians, New Generation). Generalisation about such (often nebulous) groups is fraught with difficulties, but it nevertheless holds that in each case the typical poem is a closed, monolineal utterance, demanding little of the reader but passive consumption. Such a cultural vision has obviously been privileged not simply by the major publishing houses, but also by their attendant infrastructures of reviewing journals, "literaries" and other elements of the media. The "mainstream" is, for most of the United Kingdom population, for most of the time, the only perceptible stream.

This collection is therefore oppositional to much of that mainstream. It shows a range of other approaches to poetry that have been practiced in the

British Isles over the last quarter century, and that reflect and contribute to a different understanding of that world. Each one of the poetries represented has been carefully and deliberately arrived at by its proponents, and diligently pursued over a sustained period—yet for the most part these writings remain more or less completely outside the broadly recognised cultural hierarchies of Britain and Ireland, with only a handful receiving any of the recognition and critical attention which is their due.

Of course, in many cases, this "neglect" is hardly surprising, since the writers concerned would not seek—or have indeed formally rejected—inclusion into existing hierarchies, which they see as increasingly lifeless and irrelevant. Significantly, one poet/editor comments on dominant work immediately prior to our period as having a "depthless vision of the past."[1] Others have perceived such cultural institutions as at best diversive, and at worst corrupting, serving only to prop wider hierarchies of power or wealth—no accident, in this adversarial context, that when Rupert Murdoch's media empire News International took over the Collins publishing group, an early priority was to close the Paladin Poetry series (in which a number of the most innovative writers featured here had appeared), destroying much of the remaining stock. And others, marginalised for one reason or another from a dominant orthodoxy, simply wanted no truck with it.

Neglect, however, is not a new phenomenon in the literature of the Britain and Ireland: the "discovery" of Basil Bunting at the age of sixty-five is now well enough known to stand as lasting reproof to British literary circles, and his career is certainly an exemplar for much of this collection. There are several poets included here whose work has remained unread longer than it ought: Jonathan Griffin, known only to a discerning few in his lifetime, saw his work collected in two volumes in the United States in the year of his death; Brian Coffey in Ireland is still in great need of re-editing and collecting some years after his death. These are not isolated instances.

By avoiding—or being avoided by—the mainstream of literary culture, many of these writers retain a freedom to develop as they wish, and have made good use of this freedom. They have been made to confront the very nature of their texts in order to disseminate them all. The importance of small presses and magazines in this process is so widely recognised as to need little further discussion here: suffice it to say that a range of diverse and changing small presses, operating with a minimum of resource and a high amount of commitment, has enabled much of the work here to find its informed audiences, to pass beyond the shores of Britain and Ireland, and to form meaningful links with other makers and other literatures. In addition, many of the writers here are or have been publishers themselves: this self-empowerment has been crucial to the independence of the poetries presented. What is less frequently acknowledged is the equal importance—here as elsewhere in the past—of the oral presence of these texts. Poetry performances—in a wide range of styles and circumstances—have played a significant part in the development of this work, foregrounding patterns of regional, local, and individual speech. By such means have pluralities within communities resisted marginalisation within the culture while enriching it.

They have not all been entirely neglected, of course, but recognition has as a rule been more generous outside the confines of Britain and Ireland. In his ground-breaking anthology 23 *Modern British Poets* (Chicago: Swallow, 1971) John Matthias reported that "there is a contemporary British poetry which is modern; for a while that seemed to be in doubt.... Too often 'British' means *old* or *tired* in America, 'contemporary' rather than 'modern,' Philip Larkin rather than Tom Raworth" (xii). But his news fell on deaf ears, especially in the British Isles. Of the poets we include in this anthology, only three are mentioned in *Poetry Today: A Critical Guide to British Poetry 1960–1995*, by Anthony Thwaite: Fred D'Aguiar, Linton Kwesi Johnson, and Tom Leonard. None of them is discussed. Thwaite was awarded on OBE (Order of the British Empire) in 1990 "for his services to poetry"; his book, advertised as "the most authoritative and up to date survey" of thirty-five years of British Poetry, went into its third revised edition in 1996. Commissioned by the British Council and co-published in London by Longman, Thwaite's book might legitimately be read as representing the dominant "mainstream" view. In none of its three editions does his book mention such remarkable long modernist works as Brian Coffey's *Advent* (1975), or the work of Basil Bunting (1900–1985), W. S. Graham (1918–1986), and Jonathan Griffin (1906–1990), all actively and influentially writing and publishing through the sixties and seventies. The book takes no cognizance of ambitious projects like Allen Fisher's *Place* project from the 1970s or Robert Sheppard's ongoing *Twentieth Century Blues*. As Maurice Scully has noted, there is a "completely buried 'modernist/experimental' tradition."

The tradition of which Scully speaks is long, dissenting, and largely disregarded if not indeed suppressed. Its history has yet to be written, and stretches back to Clare, Blake, Smart, and the two Vaughans, Henry and Thomas. It is a tradition that in this century has not been ashamed to borrow from overseas models (such as Apollinaire, Horace, Rudaki, or Whitman), and that runs counter to the mainstreams of British verse. Pointing to one thread of that tradition, Basil Bunting used to say of the thirty years 1920–1950 that they were "the American years," and would talk of the great American poets, Niedecker, Pound, William Carlos Williams, and Zukofsky, limiting his esteem for Eliot, and only excepting from what he called the doldrums of English poetry in those decades the work of David Jones, Hugh MacDiarmid, and (with some diffidence) himself. Bunting's estimate (whatever we may think of it) points to two things: an (urgent) felt need to turn to foreign-language models (and a re-evaluation of "classical" literatures), and an insistence—as evidenced in his three exceptions—on the worth of the local and regional: Jones the Anglo-Welsh Londoner, MacDiarmid the nationalist and Marxist Scot, and himself, the Northumbrian who kept his very specific west-of-Newcastle speech throughout his life. "We have all been driven," he said, "to use some approximation to standard English, a koiné, nobody's native tongue."[2]

Such suspicion of standardization and uniformity is reflected in the title of this book, which avoids the adjectival implications of the definite and indefinite article. "An Other" implies a kind of random harmony, but it is extremely difficult, if not impossible, to formulate a single statement that would hold true for all the writers in this book, beyond the probability that they all share a lack of interest in the work of their well-established "mainstream" contemporaries. Although each practices an oppositional poetics, there is no common politics of poetic form, nor is there of opposition, and their unity as a group is largely notional. "The Other" implies the encyclopaedic and exhaustive, which this book clearly is not. It is worth noting that this book does not include work from the vigorous and innovative Gaelic Scots revival, nor from the Welsh; there is no work here by, for instance, the urban Punjabi Scot or the rural African English. A list of some significant omissions, restricted to a length similar to inclusions, is worth giving for readers to pursue elsewhere: Gilbert Adair, Asa Benveniste, Caroline Bergvall, Jean "Binta" Breeze, Paul Brown, Jim Burns, Brian Catling, David Chaloner, Miles Champion, Paula Claire, Merle Collins, Simon Cutts, David Dabydeen, Andrew Duncan, G. F. Dutton, Paul Evans, Ian Hamilton Finlay, Glenda George, Harry Guest, Robert Hampson, Ralph Hawkins, David Haynes, W. N. Herbert, Paul Holman, Dom Sylvester Houedard, Mark Hyatt, Grace Lake, Peter Larkin, Tim Longville, Brian Marley, D. S. Marriott, Rod Mengham, Peter Middleton, David Miller, Drew Milne, Edwin Morgan, Koef Nielsen, Stephen Oldfield, Out To Lunch, Ian Patterson, Simon Pettet, Frances Presley, J. H. Prynne, Michele Roberts, Lemn Sissay, Hazel Smith, Ken Smith, Geoffrey Squires, Ian Stephen, Janet Sutherland, Levi Tafari, Harriet Tarlo, Fiona Templeton, Nick Totton, Michelin Wandor, Eugene Watters, John Wilkinson, Aaron Williamson—and others. All of these writers reflect a number of overlapping zones of concern, including (severally but not universally, and in widely disparate ways) class, race, gender, creed; and interests, regional, political, economic, or aesthetic. The ironies latent in that "Other" are in any case echoed in the "British" and "Irish" complications in the title of this book. Randolph Healy considers himself an Irish poet, and has lived in Ireland most of his life, but he was born in Scotland. Billy Mills and Catherine Walsh are insistent that they not be considered "English" or "British," but for most of their writing careers before 1996 they lived in the south of England and, earlier, in Barcelona. They belong, perhaps, to the long tradition of self-exile among Irish writers, one shared by Brian Coffey (living in Southampton after lengthy domicile in France) and Maurice Scully (now living in Ireland, but for some years in Greece and Lesotho). "Britain" at a simplistic geographic level includes Wales, Scotland, and Northern Ireland. Most of the poets in this anthology are English, but each will understand this in a different context, and most will reject the stylised anglophilia of, say, Geoffrey Hill or Philip Larkin.

*

Estonian poet Jaan Kaplinski has identified a syndrome of "Wandering Border" that is not irrelevant here, for the problem of national identity is complex indeed. The twentieth century has seen an extraordinary expansion of mobility, in a populace drenched if not drowning in the sheer quantity not only of its own numbers but also of material goods and information. The wide accessibility of mass transit systems, and the often brutal and desperate pressures of political and military coercion and/or economic necessity, have established and sanctioned an extraordinary polyglot and diverse cultural mix of urban sprawl and migrant labour on all six continents. "Foreign populations," as ethnographer James Clifford puts it in *The Predicament of Culture,* "have come to stay — mixing in but often in partial, specific fashions. The 'exotic' is uncannily close."[3] Under such circumstances, what sort of behaviour can be considered "truly English," what form of identity can "properly" be characterized as "Irish"? Can any behaviour — whether seven thousand miles away or in the house next door — meaningfully be called "exotic"? Can it, for that matter, be called "normal"? These are crucial questions that affect literary as well as political and social behaviours and values. For if an older experience of identity can no longer be affirmed, if an earlier distinctness of unified "culture" can no longer be asserted, then the artistic as well as linguistic, ethical, and religious traditions associated with them can no longer serve as indices of national identity or authenticity. The twentieth century has forcefully and often brutally reminded itself that ethnic purity is no guarantee of "identity," and is a chimaera: the nineteenth-century "English" cannot be "the same" as those of the fourteenth.

Terms like "British," "English," or "Irish" begin to transcend ethnic origin or significance; they are instead geographical terms with local rather than "cultural" extensions and implications. In most cases they serve as markers of place of residence or birth; they help to identify a "voice." In very important ways — ways generally unthinkable in Victorian England, and certainly shunned if at all raised in English literary circles in the first half of this century — one's identity may have become, like one's loyalties, a matter of personal necessity. This has surprising, and even shocking consequences. Globally, the closing years of this century have witnessed a substantial number of land claims by supposedly "extinct" indigenous peoples and re-assertions of identity; there has been a surprising recovery of "lost" traditions, customs, languages, and even political and judicial systems over a large part of the globe. Identity, and the "culture" that goes with it, is conjectural, invented and inventive, not intrinsic — this is the age of mestizo culture, of mixtures, of (in Clifford's phrasing) an "unprecedented overlay of traditions" (9). In any community multiple-identity structures are in play. Communities overlap and intertwine, are local and spread out, tight-knit and fragmented, in a way that Langland could hardly have predicted but to which he was, in fact, no stranger.

Such a situation calls for a poetics of displacement, but such a poetics takes multiple forms. One response is to embrace a species of dislocated language and reading praxis. "Maybe it's because I've been living outside the UK for 21 years," Tony Frazer (editor of Shearsman Books and *Shearsman* magazine) has said, "but it seems to me irrelevant where you come from. The interesting thing is poetry in English, whatever its port of origin: I happily read Australian poets, Canadians, Americans, Brits, Irish—there's a difference of tone I grant you, but not much more." Yet Frazer's own editing practice, in the pages of *Shearsman*, by no means reflects earlier or mainstream notions of the transcendent Work-of-Art, for the writers he publishes (many of them included in this book) are often intensely focussed on the immediate and the local. To those unused to such writing strategies, such work may look fragmented and incomplete, be unsatisfying because it shuns reaching conclusions or adumbrating a wholeness of vision. But the conditions to which such work is a response are global as well as local; it is a poetry of dislodgement. Meditating upon his own position as a Palestinian writer, historian, and critic, Edward Said suggests that

A part of something is for the foreseeable future going to be better than all of it. Fragments over wholes. Restless nomadic activity over the settlements of held territory. Criticism over resignation. . . . Attention, alertness, focus. To do as others do, but somehow to stand apart. To tell your story in pieces, *as it is*.[4]

Tell it as it is, not so much claiming an identity for political reasons (though clearly the political has an important role) as positioning the self in a shifting world of continual change, of complex and intensely problematised hybridities and polyglossia, characterized by a kind of voluntary tribalisation that is suspicious of all external claims to authority or authenticity.

Power structures rest upon claims to transcendent identity and unity, and in laying claim to the universality of moral, ethical, and aesthetic values they deny their own historical contingency. They install centrist monologic utterance as the norm. It is the nature of power to hold to concepts of Absolute Reality, through which it controls, and to which it claims to be obedient: Necessity; Justice; Morality; Intelligibility; Art. Whatever these grand concepts might mean (Robert Musil called them "luminously vacuous"), in one aspect of their existence they are all subsumed under the concept of established centralised tradition.

It is important to remember here that tradition, as instrument of power, sanctions agreed habits of syntax, rhythms and sequences of thought, intonation, figurative language, and range of diction. The normative impulses of literary and linguistic tradition reinforce notions of intelligibility (and of syntax) that themselves constitute the intellectual legitimation of political rule, of the hegemony, whose very existence resides in and relies upon its moral and cultural legitimation by tradition, if it is not to be installed and maintained by power of brute force. Its vocabulary prizes terms like "unified" and "centred," for in proposing their contraries—edges, margins, fragments—such terms trivialise and thus silence dissent. They thus iron out diversity and multiplicity by dividing the world into such binaries as us and them, real and unreal, authentic and fake, original and imitation, true and false, poet and poetaster, and shift the attention away from the local, toward the centre. The poets collected here, without exception, resist centrality. In doing so, many have become associated with concepts of "avant garde" or "experimentalism," but these terms are of little help in perceiving the work, or the primary drive within it.

Allen Fisher has spoken of the need "to realise the potentials whilst holding on to where we are"—like Said, then, and like many of the poets in this book, embracing the local, the what-is-to-hand in the where-we-are. But what, exactly, is to hand, and where exactly is this where-we-are? "I need interactions and they lead to selection and I deal with selections and not everything," Fisher remarked on e-mail of his work, which draws on an astonishing range of materials, from pop culture to "high art" and highly technical theory. He has discussed the problems one must face up to in an attempt "to live with quantity": selection, choice, identity, value—what Fisher calls "patterns of connectedness"—all demand a close and indeed stringent attention not only to whatever artifact the where-we-are world might offer to hand, but to the circumstances of its production and the necessity of its retention, in an attempt to experience its immediacy in historical as well as in immediately contemporary terms.

You don't descend on Majiayao culture (in neolithic China) and run off with the shiny bits, but hold in there to attempt a better understanding of where it is and who did this or that, and then leave it intact—rested in the pleasure of what it was that happened when you were there.

Living in the world is a demanding and scrupulous business.

Avoiding the voyeuristic pleasures of the spectator and the touristic entertainments of appropriation, telling it as it is, Fisher's view of the local extends beyond immediate geographical, social, or temporal limits and chimes with a tradition leading back to Clare. He has suggested that we start to experience the planet as local only when we see "migrations of image and understanding," citing as examples "the coriolis spin the positions in star fields the similarity and differences in plantlife." This is, then, a poetics of memory and invention, of selection and surprise, and Fisher's interrogation and redefinition of the where-we-are finds an apt counterpoint in Cris Cheek's very different e-mail reflections on the what it means to embrace local values:

Here, in Lowestoft, I live—am regularly in Norwich (several days each week), when I'm not teaching in Devon or touring either here or in mainland Europe, or visiting London or Cambridge or Liverpool or Derby (just some of which are on a regular network for me) and so on. Let alone in this e-place, that partially conflates distance between Leamington Spa and Detroit. . . . I am not from Lowestoft, having spent most of my life until 3 years back in the big smoke. I will probably never be considered a "Lowestoftian," and will never lose, let alone seek to erase, my London experiences—they're hard-wired into the psychic circuitry.

The high mobility characterizing Cheeks' experience is not itself unusual, but it is hard to see the relevance to it of such terms as "unified" or "centred"—neither is it precisely "nomadic." Older terminologies, that is to say, and older distinctions and binaries, begin to break down. One would be hard-pressed to consider Cheek's or Fisher's work in terms of its "solidity"—a critical term much favoured by critics like James Fenton and Anthony Thwaite—just as one would have great difficulty praising the work of Ken Edwards, Linton Kwesi Johnson, or Catherine Walsh for the "delectability" of its language. The aloof condescension implicit in especially these two terms shapes experience to established measures; it is characteristic of a world view that values well-established norms, and upholds constants of perfection. Life goes on the even tenor of its way, unflurried and unruffled in its stable predictability.

*

One purpose of this anthology is therefore to uncover what the forces surrounding The Movement and its successors have helped to bury. Dominating as they have the major organs of culture, they stifled the impact of the likes of Cobbing and Raworth—to say nothing of countless others—for thirty years, driving the Other underground by virtue of simply defining them as Other. They found William Carlos Williams unreadable or overrated (his work was not published in Britain until 1963, and then by the upstart publishing house of McGibbon and Kee),[5] scorned Black Mountain writers like Creeley, Duncan, and especially Olson, and continue to deride the $L=A=N=G=U=A=G=E$ poets and their relations. What interest they take in writing from the broad linguistic diaspora is confined to American writers such as Amy Clampitt, Derek Walcott, and C. K. Williams, with John Ashbery and Allen Ginsberg as token (and scorned) radicals, and European poetries pursued largely for political ends.

Starting in the 1950s an increasing number of young British poets turned away from the mainstream of English writing, by and large rejecting the insularity and bland humanism of the dominant mainstream, turning to foreign models: Brian Coffey translating French, Jonathan Griffin translating Portuguese, modernist writing; Prynne reading Celan and Rilke; Harwood translating Tzara and opening communication with surviving Dadaists. Founding their own little magazines, publishing not only their own but also imported poetry, these poets turned especially but not only to American models. As travel restrictions relaxed, they moved overseas (as did Gael Turnbull to Canada and the United States to train as a doctor); as currency restrictions eased, they imported texts from other cultures. Olson and Zukofsky read in London; Prynne and Dorn did a reading tour together of North America.

*

It is of course an extreme oversimplification, but it is nevertheless quite useful to suggest that many of the writers in this anthology regard Bob Cobbing, Eric Mottram, and J. H. Prynne as forebears as much as contemporaries. Other names, notably Andrew Crozier, Ian Hamilton Finlay, Roy Fisher, and Gael Turnbull, might arguably replace these, for they too by their example and activity opened up new opportunities for British and Irish poetry. Behind all six writers, of course, are those of an earlier generation, Basil Bunting, David Jones, and Hugh MacDiarmid, who themselves found great intellectual, thematic, and especially technical and formal resource in the work of such American modernists as T. S. Eliot, Ezra Pound, William Carlos Williams, and Gertrude Stein. As we've already noted, one sign of the urgency the writers of an earlier generation felt is that in their insistent demand for a poetry that would, in Bunting's words, "escape from the hampering measures imposed by our memory of several centuries of English verse written by models imported from other lands,"[6] they would themselves turn to foreign writers as examples and source. It would be misleading, however, to speak of any of these writers in terms of any simplistic influence: Louis Zukofsky (whose name also belongs in the tutelary roster) spoke of "an influence acting in common upon individual temperaments" according to "1. its presence in the air . . . ; 2. coincidence . . . ; 3. conscious choice or rejection of a literary tradition."[7] Thus Gael Turnbull, living in Canada, the United States, and the United Kingdom, worked with Roy Fisher and Michael Shayer to publish American poets like Edward Dorn as well as radical younger British writers (including Finlay and Fisher) under their Migrant imprint, and also published *Migrant*, a magazine that gave its readers access to work by American writers such as Robert Creeley, Denise Levertov, and Charles Olson. A little later Andrew Crozier prepared an edition of the poetry of Carl Rakosi, American Objectivist poet of the 1930s, for his doctorate at the State University of New York at Buffalo. Finlay published books by Lorine Niedecker and Louis Zukofsky under the Wild Hawthorn Press imprint, as well as radical younger British and North American writers in his little magazine *P.O.T.H. (Poor Old Tired Horse)*, and—through his own example and in his extensive correspondence with other poets—played an important role (as did Hugh MacDiarmid, his fellow Scot with whom he quarreled bitterly) in the strong Scottish revival of the 1950s on, and, later, gave enormous impetus to the redefinition as well as production of concrete poetry, which lies in general outside the scope of this book.

However, as editors, writers, publishers, and teachers (whether or not in an institutional setting), and indeed as promoters, Cobbing, Mottram, and Prynne played central strategic roles in the 1970s and 1980s—decades in which poets of the Other, through readings, festivals, and an astonishing proliferation of little magazines and small presses, became increasingly aware of each other's work and began to acquire a sense that they were collectively developing some of the issues and positions they had inherited from the 1960s counterculture—indeed, that they had themselves helped formulate in what Robert Sheppard has called that decade's "utopia of dissent."[8] Cobbing, a resourceful and tireless arts and workshop organizer and publisher, established his radical press Writers Forum in 1954, in 1963 putting its output on a more established and consistent footing, producing cheap mimeographed pamphlets of experimental writing and concrete poetry with great persistence. In his own work he was developing the fusion of visual and aural performance elements that make him a consistent force within British poetry. His re-defining of the nature of the "text"—as shown by work in this anthology—remains extreme and radical today. Much of the work of Writers Forum, when it was not Cobbing's own (for instance, Lee Harwood's so-called *title illegible* [1965]), emerged from his regular workshops, and by 1970 Writers Forum had produced 54 titles.[9] In the 1960s, too, Cobbing had been active in the promotion of the Association of Little Presses (devoted to issues related to funding, production, and distribution) and produced regular checklists and bibliographies of recent small press publications. Cobbing drew poets to him through his association with Better Books, an important London place for poetry readings and a well-resourced library (as was Tom Pickard's bookshop Ultima Thule, in Newcastle, for a different group of poets), and his activities on behalf of an alternative poetics got renewed impetus, energy, and powers with his election in the early 1970s to the General Council of the Poetry Society.

Until the 1970s the Poetry Society, a long-established but more-or-less obsolete national institution based in London and comfortably funded by the Arts Council, devoted most of its energies to its small library in London, running of poetry-reading contests throughout the British school system, the selection and distribution of the "Poetry Society Book Choice" each month to its members, the sponsorship of occasional poetry readings, and the publication of its house journal, *Poetry Review*. In 1971, as part of an organizational and political coup for a poetics of dissent and dislocation, Basil Bunting became President of the Poetry Society and Eric Mottram took over the editorship of *Poetry Review* (a position he held until 1977), and by 1975 radical poets had gained a majority of seats on the General Council. A series of radical reforms followed: regular workshops; readings and experimental performances (Cobbing encouraging young performance poets Cris Cheek and Lawrence Upton, for example); the establishment of a print room and a book shop with an wide-ranging and eclectic stock; and a regular series of "Poetry Information" interview evenings in which Eric Mottram publicly documented alternative poetries. Some of these interviews were later broadcast on BBC radio or were published in Peter Hodgkiss's invaluable magazine *Poetry Information* (which also, until its demise in 1980, published checklists and catalogues of small press publishing activities as well as reviews and essays on little-known writers). Under Mottram's editorship *Poetry Review* published work by well-established and by new or little-known writers, as well as by a number of American poets whose work was hard to come by in Britain, such as Robert Creeley, Robert Duncan, Charles Olson, George Oppen, and Gary Snyder.

The Arts Council, meanwhile, attempted to exercise control over the Poetry Society and to oust Mottram from his editorship. Many poets resigned from the General Council in protest in 1977, and the Association of Little Presses (through Bob Cobbing and Bill Griffiths) in 1977 and 1978 documented that the Arts Council was now turning down funding applications from poets and presses associated with the Poetry Society during these years. Mottram's and Cobbing's activities in these years had enormous impact upon the possibilities open to young writers; their effect upon many of the poets included in this book is inestimable. Equally inestimable, perhaps, is Mottram's effect as Lecturer (subsequently Reader, and Professor of American Literature) at King's College, University of London, where he taught from 1971 to 1990, influencing generations of London poets such as Bill Griffiths, Ken Edwards, Allen Fisher, and Robert Sheppard. As lecturer and critic Mottram indefatigably introduced an English audience to work by neglected modernist British and more-or-less unknown contemporary American writers: Basil Bunting, Roy Fisher, David Jones, Gael Turnbull; Robert Creeley, Edward Dorn, Robert Duncan, Charles Olson, and Louis Zukofsky, among others. He also tirelessly furthered the work of emerging English contemporaries such as Colin Simms, Tom Pickard, and Barry MacSweeney, and actively supported many little magazines like *Talus*, founded and edited by students and colleagues at King's College. It is worth remarking that many of those who worked with Mottram in London also attended Bob Cobbing's workshops: for all their self-evident differences, the work of these two major source-figures clearly complemented each other.

So, in a rather different way, did that of J. H. Prynne, from his position in Cambridge: the spell he cast upon his contemporaries and subsequent generations of readers and writers bears what is now understood to be a "Cambridge" flavour (though the boundaries are notoriously hard to draw). In the 1960s Prynne was the centre of a group of young writers in Cambridge (including Andrew Crozier, Veronica Forrest-Thomson, John James, Wendy Mulford, John Riley, and Peter Riley) who shared awareness of contemporary American and European poets. During this decade and into the 1970s a flurry of little magazines appeared from this group, including *The English Intelligencer* (edited by

Crozier and Prynne), *Grosseteste Review* (Tim Longville and John Riley), *Outburst* (Tom Raworth), and *Resuscitator* (John James). Since the 1960s Prynne has in addition had an enduring and powerful effect as teacher (of Rod Mengham and Tony Lopez among others) and presenter of non-English language poetries, and has in both formal and informal ways been a focus for an extraordinarily active and changing group of writers living not only in Cambridge but also overseas. In the 1960s Prynne's own special interests were in contemporary German poetry—on which he is a considerable authority—and the work of Black Mountain poets, especially Charles Olson, about whose *Maximus Poems IV, V, VI* he wrote an important early review essay, published in Crozier's magazine *The Park*.[10] In the late 1960s he undertook an extensive reading tour of Canada and the United States with Edward Dorn, who was at that time working at the University of Essex, and his own poetry at the end of the 1960s—collected in *The White Stones* (1969)—takes up the challenge Black Mountain poetics offered. Dorn's essay *What I See in the Maximus Poems*, published as a pamphlet by Gael Turnbull's Migrant press in 1960, along with Prynne's own review of Olson's long poem in process, emphasized the necessity, as Robert Sheppard has put it, to withdraw from the oppositional politics of the 1960s in order to ground individual consciousness in the concreteness of immediate experience, and offered a strategy whereby poets might slough off the abstractions of a thoughtless and unfeeling because conventional humanist ideology of a political nation and a notional British identity.

The great attraction of Olson's poetics was, first, its insistence (following perhaps the lead of Thoreau) that intelligence is inseparable from the whole range of immediate, physical, bodily perception; second, that the mind pay close attention to the perceptual rather than the conceptual field (or, as William Carlos Williams put it for an earlier generation of American poets, to what lies under the nose); and third—as corollary—that the immediacies of local history and geography (beginning with the body, even) are the only source and ground of knowledge, action, and use. This attack upon conventional and unconscious ideologies that Prynne, Mottram, Cobbing and others saw as vitiating an enervated post-war British culture played its part in freeing British writers, as it freed Olson, into a species of improvisational poetics in which "ONE PERCEPTION MUST IMMEDIATELY AND DIRECTLY LEAD TO A FURTHER PERCEPTION" (Edward Dahlberg's words, adopted by Olson).[11] At the same time, Olson's own preoccupations with the historical origins of a twentieth-century malaise led him—and poets like Allen Fisher in his long serial poem of the 1970s, *Place*, and Prynne in *The White Stones*—to the detailed and passionate investigation (often in notational form) of local history and geography, taking as starting point Heraclitus's pre-Socratic dictum, "Man is estranged from that with which he is most familiar," and to the development of a language that is an action upon the real rather than a discourse of abstractions (taxonomies, idealizations) about it. In Fisher's and Prynne's hands, a principal task of the poem is to disrupt reader's automatic response to language by making language itself the source of experience in the poem. The concomitant disruptions relocate politics within everyday experience.

Overall, such work opened up the possibility of an open poetry of exploration and even interrogation characterized by a play of possible meanings, rather than by the enunciation of a meaning forwarded by thesis, and initiated the gradual formulation of meaning as a construction of the reader's rather than of the writer's. This is the antithesis of the "mainstream" poem principle demonstrated earlier. Under no circumstances can the poem be considered the small-scale artifact, crafted according to the precepts of an abstract idealized perfection. With such a possibility, a deeply ethical concern becomes a necessity. In Allen Fisher's case, the poem is developed through recourse to procedures and systems in which material (and meaning) is generated by apparently random methods; the boundaries of the poem itself are fluid, since a single section might be part of more than one work, and the numbered parts of the poem might themselves be read in any order. Fisher is seeking a form that readers can enter at any point, and in which they can move, draw connections, find correspondences and contradictions, as their own experience of the text makes possible — it is not necessary, that is to say, to have a *complete* text, for the poem itself is continually changing and is largely without bounds. In 1975 by his own count Fisher was involved in thirty-four projects, including collages, found texts, mail art, dream poems, experiments in music and art, as well as performance; by 1995 his published works (pamphlets, books, tapes, and records) numbered over one hundred — an output perhaps paralleled by Bob Cobbing's enormous production of sound and visual concrete poetry.

By around 1970 these differing forces appeared to have attained a brief homogeneity under the unlikely tag of "underground" poetry, as exemplified in Michael Horovitz's anthology *Children of Albion: Poetry of the "Underground" in Britain* (Harmondsworth: Penguin, 1969), and in a visible surge of middle-sized presses edited and/or run by poets such as Cape Editions (Nathaniel Tarn), Ferry (Andrew Crozier), Fulcrum (Stuart Montgomery), Goliard (Tom Raworth), Migrant (Turnbull), and Trigram (Asa Benveniste), which ensured some accessibility of texts. Poetry-reading venues had sprung up around the country, at once ensuring that poets had some visibility, and that part of the poetic "push" (in writers as different as Harwood and Turnbull, for instance) was oral, within a tradition of voiced poetry. It is no accident that one of the most prominent reading venues of the time was the Morden Tower in Newcastle, founded by Connie and Tom Pickard under the aegis of Basil Bunting, and fusing the emerging "Other" British poets with a stream of visiting Americans. Although such prominence was (a) short-lived and (b) more apparent than actual, it did establish reference points for subsequent development: a number of the "younger" poets included here had their introductions to poetry at this time. Although the presses fell prey to economics and personal circumstance, and the alliances (implied more in anthologists' tags than in reality) dissolved as the individuals developed, a new reader coming to "non-mainstream" British poetry in the early 1970s could find reference points to relate to.

Such reference points shift, of course, over time—witness such collections as *Ten British Poets*, Ian Sinclair's three short-lived "Re/Active Anthologies," and his subsequent collection *Conductors of Chaos*.[12] The poetry we have gathered in this book is exploratory and developmental, presented over a developmental period, and can seldom be tied to a rigid poetic: a poem from the early part of the period may not work in the same way as a more recent one. Throughout the 1970s and 1980s more elements were being added to the basic "mix" and existing associations of voices were separating out, to be heard individually. The United Kingdom's ethnic diversity already referred to began at this stage to produce rich poetries loaded with overt criticism of dominant white culture, and making innovative use of dub and rap traditions in ways that others were quick to appreciate and absorb. The experimental legacy of sixties art movements such as Fluxus began to be felt in a number of the more openly experimental writers, and as the 1980s moved into the 1990s so-called Language Poetry began to enrich the mix, extending the resources of the poem without compromising its insistence on the local and immediate. And from the interplays of (say) Bob Cobbing's sound poetry and Linton Kwesi Johnson's work emerged a renewed interest in performance, in sounded poetry, which can perhaps be traced back to Bunting (Maggie O'Sullivan traces her own concerns in that way). This element is, of course, lost in a printed collection, but as these threads multiply and grow stronger we can only affirm that the oral tradition of poetry, proclaimed repeatedly by Bunting, has become a poetic fact of today.

Finally, as editors we may record with pleasure our thanks to all those who have helped and encouraged us in making this book—a project which has its origins in discussions in many places over many years. All "our" authors, of course, without whom the book would have been thin indeed, have been a pleasure to work with, and three—Fred D'Aguiar, Hany Gilonis, and Bill Griffiths—have also contributed a range of editorial help and advice without which the book would have been poorer. The staff of Wesleyan University Press and the University Press of New England have been consistent in the level of constructive help and support throughout: Eileen McWilliam, who as Director of Wesleyan University Press was the first to believe in the book, deserves our special thanks. She passed on her enthusiasm to Suzanna Tamminen who as Editor in Chief saw the project to conclusion with a level of creativity and sympathy which has made the work a pleasure. Editorial and design staff have been of a consistent high quality, rising magnificently to the challenges of encompassing the diverse range of stylistic requirements presented here. Antony Gormley gave his permission freely for the use of his amazing *Field for the British Isles* for our cover. And Ann Caddel and Meredith Quartermain put up with an astounding range of preoccupation and obsession to more than justify the dedication of the book.

Richard Caddel and Peter Quartermain

NOTES

1. Andrew Crozier, "Introduction," *A Various Art*, ed. Andrew Crozier and Tim Longville (Manchester: Carcanet, 1987) 12.
2. Basil Bunting, "The Use of Poetry," *Writing* 12 (Summer 1985): 42.
3. James Clifford, *The Predicament of Culture: Twentieth-Century Ethnography, Literature, and Art* (Cambridge: Harvard UP, 1988) 13.
4. Edward Said, *After the Last Sky: Palestinian Lives* (New York: Pantheon, 1986) 150 (Said's italics).
5. There was also a small (500-copy) edition of *Paterson* Books 1 & 2 published in 1953 by Peter Owen, who had bought the sheets from New Directions.
6. Bunting, "1910–1920," TS lecture given at University of Newcastle upon Tyne, 1968, p. 10. (TS in the possession of Peter Quartermain.)
7. Louis Zukofsky, "Influence," *Prepositions: The Collected Critical Essays*, expanded ed. (Berkeley, U of California P, 1981) 135.
8. Robert Sheppard, "Artifice and the Everyday World: Poetry in the 1970s," *The Arts in the 1970s: Cultural Closure?*, ed. B. Moore-Gilbert (London: Routledge, 1994) 130.
9. Robert Sheppard, "British Poetry and Its Discontents," *Cultural Revolution? The Challenge of the Arts in the 1960s*, ed. B. Moore-Gilbert and John Seed (London: Routledge, 1992) 166.
10. J. H. Prynne, "[Review of] Charles Olson, *Maximus Poems IV, V, VI*," *The Park*, 4/5 (Summer 1969): 64–66.
11. Charles Olson, "Projective Verse," *Selected Writings* (New York: New Directions, 1966) 17.
12. *Ten British Poets* (Peterborough: Spectacular Diseases, 1993); *Conductors of Chaos: A Poetry Anthology*, ed. I. Sinclair (London: Picador, 1996). There were three titles in the "Re/Active Anthology" series edited by Sinclair (London: Paladin, 1992–1993).

Other

John Agard

Half-caste

Excuse me
standing on one leg
I'm half-caste

Explain yuself
wha yu mean
when yu say half-caste
yu mean when picasso
mix red an green
is a half-caste canvas/
explain yuself
wha yu mean
when yu say half-caste
yu mean when light an shadow
mix in de sky
is a half-caste weather/
well in dat case
england weather
nearly always half-caste
in fact some o dem cloud
half-caste till dem overcast
so spiteful dem dont want de sun pass
ah rass/
explain yuself
wha yu mean
when you say half-caste
yu mean when tchaikovsky
sit down at dah piano
an mix a black key
wid a white key
is a half-caste symphony/

Explain yuself
wha yu mean
Ah listening to yu wid de keen

half of mih ear
Ah lookin at yu wid de keen
half of mih eye
an when I'm introduced to you
I'm sure you'll understand
why I offer yu half-a-hand
an when I sleep at night
I close half-a-eye
consequently when I dream
I dream half-a-dream
an when moon begin to glow
I half-caste human being
cast half-a-shadow
but yu must come back tomorrow

wid de whole of yu eye
an de whole of yu ear
an de whole of yu mind

an I will tell yu
de other half
of my story

Palm Tree King

Because I come from the West Indies
certain people in England seem to think
I is a expert on palm trees

So not wanting to sever dis link
with me native roots (know what ah mean?)
or to disappoint dese culture vulture
I does smile cool as seabreeze

and say to dem
which specimen
you interested in
cause you talking
to the right man
I is palm tree king
I know palm tree history

like de palm o me hand
In fact me navel string
bury under a palm tree

If you think de queen could wave
you ain't see nothing yet
till you see the Roystonea Regia
— that is the royal palm —
with she crown of leaves
waving calm-calm
over the blue Caribbean carpet
nearly 100 feet of royal highness

But let we get down to business
Tell me what you want to know
How tall a palm tree does grow?
What is the biggest coconut I ever see?
What is the average length of the leaf?

Don't expect me to be brief
cause palm tree history
is a long-long story

Anyway why you so interested
in length and circumference?
That kind of talk so ordinary
That don't touch the essence
of palm tree mystery
That is no challenge
to a palm tree historian like me

If you insist on statistics
why you don't pose a question
with some mathematical profundity?

Ask me something more tricky
like if a American tourist with a camera
take 9 minutes to climb a coconut tree
how long a English tourist without a camera
would take to climb the same coconut tree?

That is problem pardner
Now ah coming harder

If 6 straw hat
and half a dozen bikini
multiply by the same number of coconut tree
equal one postcard
how many square miles of straw hat
you need to make a tourist industry?

That is problem pardner
Find the solution
and you got a revolution

But before you say anything
let I palm tree king
give you dis warning
Ah want de answer in metric
it kind of rhyme with tropic
Besides it sound more exotic

Listen Mr Oxford Don

Me not no Oxford don
me a simple immigrant
from Clapham Common
I didn't graduate
I immigrate

But listen Mr Oxford don
I'm a man on de run
and a man on de run
is a dangerous one

I ent have no gun
I ent have no knife
but mugging de Queen's English
is the story of my life

I dont need no axe
to split/ up yu syntax
I dont need no hammer
to mash/ up yu grammar

I warning you Mr Oxford don
I'm a wanted man
and a wanted man
is a dangerous one

Dem accuse me of assault
on de Oxford dictionary/
imagine a concise peaceful man like me/
dem want me serve time
for inciting rhyme to riot
but I tekking it quiet
down here in Clapham Common

I'm not a violent man Mr Oxford don
I only armed wit mih human breath
but human breath
is a dangerous weapon

So mek dem send one big word after me
I ent serving no jail sentence
I slashing suffix in self-defence
I bashing future wit present tense
and if necessary

I making de Queen's English accessory/to my offence

Tony Baker

armillaria mellea

(for Roy Fisher & John Keats)

knees on off fists and hello lute's
fullness is all I'd ask

that voice too
should be a lace

      & not always
unknottable —

"Not played for six months
my hands feel like housebricks"

        —trailing sideways
from a stump, its deceiving
forms pungent
      & plumply chunky

  plus a veil so thick
I thought it a *cortinarius*:
my mistake.

       —or think of friend Thelonius
leaping them tenths   to opposite
              extremes, jumpin'
        Jack   landing
   slap in the crack & rhythm-a-ning
clean through all such conclusions . . .

A Pavane on Mr Wray's Locations

Audrey Causey
    betwixt Titchworth

and Chidley

       possibly

   as you go
      to the nearest windmill
on the Northside of town

      (among stones)

we could not find it

          *

        above the Paper mills
       among the stones
          in the stone walk

       as by a great ditch-side
     near Stretham ferry
           Abundantly

         about the Fens
           Marsh and Chattersee
     in the Isle of Ely

          *

    see and compare: Natura
     makes no jumps
          passes

     under the wall
       near the footway on
   the back side of Clare-hall

           to extreme   only
        through a mean

          *

   we have searched
     about a gravill-pit
near the beacon

                    from Barnwell
              to the pest-houses
              we could not find it—
                                    Howbeit

         we do not deny
                    (in some osier holts
              among stones

         possibly it may grow there

                              *

le passage (Morbihan)

              is an assemblage

                    of some kind

         swept

              like marshgrass through a fissure in

         call it mind
              if you will
         it's surely tidal
                    whatever the subject
         or its encroachments the mud   sister mud

         something that has gone out on the estuarine levels
         returns, raucous
                         into the face of it, the human
              portion a heron rises over, slow dominion
         of slewed stakes,
                    hulls,
                              their refusal, borne
         out along the margins, to test the burdens
         displaced by sheer persistence

              O Lord
              I wanna cross over, let me
              cross over into campground

8

Anthony Barnett

Music of the Spheres

A finger lifted to the eye
An indecipherable mark on the parapet
The echo of a heart
An indecisive flutter.

It was strange to me
That madder should be garanza
And guarantee garanzia.

And in my moon swarm
There is no difference
Between between

And in my halfhearted
Moon swarm
Defense and beauty
Place their feet upon the stove.

To die of cultures
Always asleep and inchoate.

And in my moon swam
Petals
Glimpses and bottles.

A shadow escaped
You paid no heed
Instead
I heard the rhythm of the head.

You ran your film
The poetry of inadequate desire.

You divulged and diverged
The shadow of a boat.

Lost and caught in the moment
Unspoken outspoken voices
Visible and volatile.

Gazing at the sky
Watching the words streaming
In the one dimensional English shape
of things.

It's all accordion.

Turbulence and Tongue

Nothing escapes.
I strengthen my
head and my heart.
Slept in my eyes. I
circle you. I turn
into the sun.

*

Lost in solicitude,
windows, impressions,
blinds.

*

The mouths wear against her.
It comes over you with a sigh.
It draws you out into the semblance.

*

Here are my thoughts
in cacophony.
Childish. Gibberish.
Beauteous.

*

Infertility.
Words.
You unfortunate cookie.

*

Captivated in the
dark ages. Inactivated
sampler.

*

O circumlocution.
Once I was interested.
Things crowded into
The Theatre of Thereafter.

*

A footnote to your history.
A proposition.
A profile.

*

Scent of elderflower.
Tar. I
put my finger on it.

*

Spent under
the heat.

Critique

Picture the lost world in
lost pictures in children's
picture books.

All the time in the fretwork of the world.

I stipule.

Frantically balancing
acts.

Those worthless words
serendipity and sublime.

Richard Caddel

Against Numerology

(i) — if you spill salt, throw a
little over your shoulder, for memory

It's freezing and you try to remember June,
the garishness and wonder. Or else a song
you loved when you were young, and now
it's stale. Faces you saw in lino, little houses
they told you weren't true but they were, they
were: not the thing itself but the sense
of other and contrary things is real.

(ii) — the whitebeams

The weather down the dales.
Then they were so hungry that they struck
and kept striking. The berries
turning scarlet in the sun, the leaves,
the leaves streamed out like banners.
When they drank it was so hard
and earnest, you'd think they'd never stop.

(iii) — fighting for strangers

The decision was endorsed by committee. Ask
if my attitude is morally defensible. Ask me
if I loved you then. Now look into the black trees
dividing sky in little chunks, a strike force, a
shanty where small, idiot hungers pipe — where,
in the world, look, another cloud gone down, and
more investment would cost you an eye and ear.

(iv)—nulla rosa est

For everything you ever had stays with you
like a japanese garden, raked sand. For
folk songs are the souls of dead workers.
For the grove we met in had seven black trees
like banners, and seven is a forgotten number. For
if you lost someone you must hug their absence.
For the other half of this verse is missing.

(v)—seagulls are the souls
of dead sailors

Pull it down like a white hankie, its
anger in bedrooms, in windowframes,
fearful to be alone in its night.
Cry to wake the dead—blade
across sky, the banners legend on the wind
tossed out to sea—remember the sea
was always in your eyes on waking.

(vi)—lowlands (for ann)

Figures dancing a long way off on hills, a
dream we wandered in too freely. Waking
to long for the quiet marshy levels, salt
sea wind in our hair and the moon. Rain
in tiny shells had washed sleep from our eyes,
we cried, as if the songs had never been,
as if our weed filled hearts were cragfast still.

(vii)—the shaggy inkcaps

Autumn—before I noticed, you were gone—
like a little home dissolving on itself.
To know that loss: the pain of hunger
and of love, and in clear air
the acrid smell of bonfires. And to know
I'll find you again, soon. Each day now
I leave the house as if I'll never return.

For Tom

Dear head, four days ahead of love's day
I bring you love. Not that you lack that,
heart, or music, living far beyond stars
close in our hearts memory and moving

hard as you did then under my hand.
Never still, your humour and sharp mind
returned bright now, little carer. So I
stumble to rest missing you, not twenty.

10/2/96

Cris Cheek

Rollercoaster

that slide would be halted
to lean on, the maxim
um sequins melted in danger

street . . . down to the bone
. . . specialising, that billion

consortium, blot harbour of actions
(that) boosted jot
greater than spartan
baloney, expanding a stagnant ludic
economy to devalue the over-written
l a n d i n g

to replace we expiring to thaw
and to plunge, got the message
hit loop, fedback plumped into food
scatters portion of what
is intriguing . . . about . . . the dead transfer, of want to go bubble hurt
come to . . . the rescue of . . . Cadence

by killing rush Hope, with tree gilding plot bets
or stop, the whistling party decomposing said
her story chronicles done recent week
we purged ourselves, and drove

weak, drawn and damn hung things
on paper, pulp the young barely cope

who partly staffs coding
winding, thirsting
in the premier
could probably help
drag screaming these indigenous
foam editions from administration

choked, at least some
prevaricating intellectual goo
of the businessmen
who, hurtling to renewed depths
more of signal than allure

saw their cherished property go shrivel
and blocking
a close decision how not to interview

overnight, it's not what
you say it's low
the ammunitions
advertised on screen flip
out of sight the lights
unlike if instituted

these motives aren't spoken
because the trial has
lined up, bread

pressed down on buckled
wheels to column
votive hill

and in the end it's what
the heart will stand

pence ... dreams ... as ... waste
\ ripped from the rough
sips blown alone street
nervous wounds that walk
their soupish paths once more

what finds its way
to stick and smacks, the weald go blind
how on this earth we dive

as bumps to brilliance turn
drown, dismiss Class
this beat of innocence
Book loving once ... commence
... to find ... what? has been ... lost

in the detrital specifics

how sweet, to drop, the root, the rot
of rope, of life and love, it's not
the same ... BANG

and hand, within hands
like the leaves on a bush
beast ... how many ... avid there
... arched ... what's left
that can be loved here

wand from a young god ? a gift
of leaving, plain slipped out of sight
rent flat, from patchwork quilts
dim transfer, pilots
to share the unexpected went
to interview the author — How

I Died With All The Rest, Fled god
damn man! what's gone can, let it loose

of sickly sweet, chirupee Virtues
that stay and that cane that be seen to stay
modish, the case that stood shivering on!
in a bestseller world of new being constructed

his jungle locked up with her
dealer, a frightening place of
good purpose transported

some scholarly
practice the trade in his freeze-dried

thought, haven
had previous
what does that mean

exactly, she
worked in the blue-collar factories
translating obviated vitality

or Tracey would say

much swelling
into severely broken home

put simply, would some uttered say
community converted
for the writing of, response

to which poetry
the injured rarely catechist extent

will plow through
shares, notes that reverberate
n o w

get on line you may notice the edge of this dread
no objection to murder read closely

is loading a dice in addition, kept ringing a bell to find out
little fucker had seeped down and ransacked indigenous

still and applying hot stones, hooting outed from paste
the developing front page supplied with quotations by crop

flow
was . . . all was . . . well
e did . . . and cold feet
yet, beginning . . . to slid

loom and slate kit
eroding the yielding of dominant instruments

glam, shuttle plume sack
fog that notorious
come to the rescue
of burst

Thomas A. Clark

Five Poems

as I walked out early
into the order of things
the world was up before me
as I stepped out bravely
the very camber of the road
turned me to its purpose
it was on a morning early
I put design behind me
hear us and deliver us
to the hazard of the road
in all the anonymous places
where the couch grass grows
watch over us and keep us
to the temper of the road

our boat touches the bank
among a scent of bruised sedge
the startled heron rises
broken from his austerities
we are in a proud country
where stone chats to stone
where furze pods crackle open
grey grouse and curlews inform
keep well below the horizon
your flesh spare upon the bone
trust to flintlock and sabre
bed down among the heather
the wild fiddle music of the air
tuneless will find you anywhere

a blessing on the house
from flags to roof-tree
may its chimney never tremble
may its lintel be confirmed
a tune always in its hearth
brightness in its threshold
may its latch be lifted
may its well never fail
with fresh bread on the table
a health in every glass
a blessing on the host
a blessing on the guest
may there be trust between them
light and shade in their conversation

sit for a while on a stone
on the slope above the river
relax and let the light drain
back to the dense tree shadows
before long someone will come
and sit with you on the stone
not beside you but taking up
exactly the space you occupy
it is the one you left behind
on every journey out of yourself
transparent, weighing nothing
breathing with you when you breathe
come to take up residence again
to look out through your eyes

the shadow extends the tree
from substance to possibility
where the tree stands, it walks
while the tree talks, it is silent
it is not a part of the tree
it is not apart from the tree
it comes and goes with the sun
and offers shelter from the sun
the tree is focused in its shadow
at each moment it is at rest
though each moment may be its last
at dawn the shadow is released
and at dusk it will again become
closer to the tree than its name

Bob Cobbing

from *Beethoven Today*

soma haoma avestan haoma
soma harita hari harita
soma haoma soma soma haoma
liska harita zarr zar-d harita
liska ling chih
soma haoma avestan haoma
soma haoma girolle chanterelle
hari harita sarcostemma brevistigma
liska harita hari harita
soma haoma soma soma haoma
liska harita liska ling chih
soma haoma avestan haoma
liska harita zarr zar-d harita
hari harita liska ling chih
hari harita sarcostemma brevistigma
soma haoma soma soma haoma o
soma haoma liska harita
girolle chanterelle
soma haoma avestan haoma
soma soma haoma liska harita
liska ling chih
liska harita zarr zar-d harita
liska harita liska ling chih
soma haoma o soma haoma
soma soma haoma girolle chanterelle
soma haoma sarcostemma brevistigma
liska harita liska ling chih
liska harita hari harita
zarr zar -d harita
soma haoma soma soma haoma
o soma haoma
liska ling chih
etc

Hymn to the Sacred Mushroom

26

from *Processual Four*

from *Prosexual*

BIRD BEE

aasvogel   brolga   colibri   dickcissel

eyas   fauvette   gallinule   hagbolt

iiwi   jabiru   korora   lammergeyer

mallemuck   nelly   ossifrage   pickmaw

quelea   rotchie   shama   tinamou

umbrette   witwall   yoldring   zoozoo

Brian Coffey

The Prayers

Where it goes on   Here not anywhere
when not anywhen   Here   Now

For why go probe whose heart

Now here an inside find
brothers sisters of ours wear
in bone skin brain tissue heart
whatever   seamless garment of pain

Never here forgetting now
that forfeit Ithaca remote
of happy men

Cruel farfromit effect imposed

Free all free that cool that mild
lake swan grass isle tree
so different from outside here
at hand constant foe

The bounds live sharp black
fringe false reaches exhaust one slay
Miles beyond swamps drab summer moss
later winter leagues in driving sleet
berries none nuts none verdure none but blighted

For bound heart bolted in surcease only in recall hopeless
of sea open to home fields

Let eye roll from North to South

grey sky to meet only sand grey
vague indifferent round
matt grey fades into sky grey
close   coverall

Inside   what's inside of outside is
feel it   learn it   hang the head
stripped cyphered emptied scoured
wreck in perpetuity

Rags   trough   plank
correlatives of gratitude
for whose return to order's zone
each in place a place for each
from start to stone

Voice in ear   no question not one's own
no question in pain too pure for lies

Not what you are   it says
Enough what code you answer to

why then not attend to voice
why not tag along

slot   into frame

Triumph of failure no goal here
snatched from mundane scene
to entry only on night-shade naught
Screw them is screw self
stone patch clod lump scum
theirs lump limp lump theirs

Here each stares each
in each self stares self
knows gorge in other rise

like gorge one's own

Did one seek sign of peace
void in other greeting void in self
brain like wave would tremble
nausea

And what is wanted of one
Entry   Takeover
total draft uncurbed
of deeps like ocean
one has recoiled from

Seven ages   seven springs
Wear away wear away
peak ocean forest plain
sand marsh salt silt
wear away wear away
earth air water fire

Never end   Ever go
wear away wear away
humble humble please them do
all that is wanted
wear away wear away
with all winds die

Make all lump
wear away wear away
for starts all you know
lax make pliant make
wear away wear away
lump make limp make lump

As if the facile blue and silver shell
of dreaming day away did harden
to ceiling jet walls black grey floor
as if spacy air did shape to cubes

As if what in dusty brake bright cirque-couchant
had shone translucent to palpitating light
became flat-forked tongue squeezed from gorge
and uncurled length opaque of dusty skin

Inside become without

One excised one's fears show
One to be filled with them
goal single   them here

Seep within they would
like ivy carpet to creep on graveyard floor
Searching their scrutiny   a dry-rot
no escape from lump once begun

Then the cold to grip
cold dark like within a stone
no moving at all
one theirs them unloving
one petrified

Book-sole one would watch
uncaring stamp to crush mouth
theirs   lump   theirs

Did they enter
within no rest more
the dark one had lounged in
busy now noisy a place trafficked in

Darkest dark
one had guarded it unscanned
its voicelessness
unaddressed unbeckoning
uncertain maybe wall-border
final frontier
of hopeless stand

island all ways bounded
self-abyss and null

From without they press
surely to grind one's history
to dust mocked
rags   trough   plank
each day's unsouling toil
each night's sodden slouching sleep
eyes open focussed on pin-point scene
eyes closed veer painwards and
cramped lie

Under their mastery exercised
lump at last   bliss numb grey
no escape elsewhere
a jelly filling mould

One had not known oneself
They had known one frail
Theirs   lump   theirs

Close of action   Query none
Eyes matt   Heart matt

No stage needs setting
in hope failed at void

Escape no-when-no-where
They keep one live theirs

What hand   what care saves here

Kelvin Corcoran

Music of the Altai Mountains

Comes to us from a distance,
it's not ours but an air surrounds us
in broken, ambiguous clouds,
a voice sings four sounds simultaneously
longing for the real to start up
in classic loose cut denim;
the hills are alive, you're not fooling anyone.

The song continued a day and night,
face-up, clearing out the house,
absorbing shapes of rain and shine
the stars and remote traffic,
transcribing the garden fathers' talk,
a fox at the rubbish, a car door slam.

All you see is drawn into that closure,
there's no technique there,
no interior, instrumental light for bearings;
you think you're trading with the enemy,
the inhabitants armed to the teeth
with the culture they despise,
look straight at you and ask one question.

*

I think it's your eyes that do it,
alive like the sky flaking away
forms such as never were in nature,
these words made for your mouth
name and strip the margin
between here and the blue folder.

We go up town for clothes,
working over the white table
in purposeful music and movement,

sends these loaded terms, your steady look
out of the window into Spring take off,
the west everywhere reeling.

It looms behind plate glass
wrapped and cushioned in lace,
rank and pink, the perfumed heart.
What can you do with it?
In this heat   on the bespattered pavement.
What?   I was walking   and you

walk by the river in darkness
where the water flows with ease

*

At night an air of leaves spills
like waves of thought in darkness,
scribbles care without sight of that face;
her hand touches moving inside,
I feel the drink hit the spot
and the roads spark into the hills.
It could be a scheme, it could be a country song,
the news is out all over town;
it's my business, a bright pattern of cracks,
the white light shoots and floods our lives.

That morning cars came out of the sun,
I couldn't measure the speeds,
careering subjects released from rhetoric
smacked up against the white wall.
The birds flip from branch to branch,
their funny watery cries all around
splash and blend in garden heat.
Splayed out under the big one
I saw that morning remote traffic arrive,
real, unexceptional vehicles.

When Suzy Was

If I look up from here
glancing off the picture David sent
I can see Skorpios across the water,
owned by Onassis, empty and unvisited.

At night navigation buoys burn
five fixed points in a line,
the island is a picture of death,
a dark thought in broad daylight.

Hermes, psychopompos, took the man down,
rising beyond the private island
the Pindus mountains make no comment,
drowned in miraculous light.

                    *

For the dead I love to dance in their bodies again
the house is too small infact,
the decor rustic haute bourgeoisie
—death turns a delicate ankle
it looks like his veins need stripping:
'We could do a deal . . .' I think not,
climb over the counter, forget the books.

The trick of separating them from their lives
gets underway before I arrive,
numberless they clamour at the window:
this one thinks if only he could arrange the letters
it would make all the difference; it won't,
the matrix of dots but motes in the air.
When Suzy was a skeleton she went   rattle   rattle   rattle.

What strikes me is how flat it all looks,
despite four grown men going mental
pressing their faces into the room,
and they become four deaths: mine.
The books bake in an oven
in a frenzy of vowels sans sense;
don't pretend you hear distant music.

It's futile to confuse my girls' fatal serial song,
the empty island of a dead plutocrat
and the printing house dance;
mountains and islands rising from the sea.

In the village an old woman stares into Madeleine's eyes,
she wants to hold the young girl's face,
it is a marvel to her, she shapes the air between us;
they're face to face and the air is still.

When Suzy was a nothing, a nothing . . .

Infact the dead have names;
my mother, my father,
Stuart, who died aged 22,
my two brothers who died as babies.

They buzz like nobody's business,
they flicker against the tiny pains
—let us in, let us in;
invisible everywhere in the picture.

She used to go like this   this   this.

In the Red Book

I'd like to write one poem but darkness is down,
just one word—the water's running against me;
fingers tied in knots and eyes gone
filled heavily to the shape you see,
but one spark, lie down you stupid bugger, lie down.

✳

We kept to coastal routes, in sight of meaning
around the shores of the various world.
Held in a disc of swimming light, miles away,
a picture of the park; under spreading oak
the exiles relax at last, their children playing.

I remember in the red book a diagram,
trade patterns put food in our mouths;
those people from across the great green
at that level of sophistication inventing surplus:
you are dedicated to trade and you to magic.

Carving this seal in carnelian, a fingertip across,
dolphin accompanying other fish, will ruin my sight
—and you to magic, just different work
in a disc of swimming light.
Look. All the trees gone for ships.

Ash   Elm   Boxwood   Maple
        the pollen levels sing from a pit
Olive   Vine   and   Fig
        the land is rising to meet you
In the red book I am a small axe.

                    *

The fleet sailed from Stony Path;
the Temple, Precipice, Sphink and Fortune,
away for the Gulf boys, on the morning away:
scattering salt on the white world
all bright and sparkling in its wake.

Andrew Crozier

Loopy Dupes

Fed back to the dot
in hoped-for recoil at this point
it weighs on the wound thread
of a button worn dangling
out of its normal rectitude
a test to tired memory
drawing its assent from the code book
where the dot abruptly refuses to budge
it is joined by others which trail behind
in meaningful suspension like a cloud
about to exhibit its other side waiting
for the stars to gleam through fixedly
their light oozing all the way
along the line blotted in a crease
which cuts the sky from edge
to edge like a sheet of paper
fresh from the quire its edges
deckled beneath the fingertips
which feel around such
flat expanse spread right across
the space it takes without pause
in its pointed dead-pan mimicry
of an act repeated in ignorance
over the pacified landscape surrounded
in speech which accelerates
constriction within the cardiac
vacuum of a tube half a size too large
for a pipe but the timetable
hums in its morning routine
and toddles in its valves like
a mute trumpet or a dogwhistle
from which some sweet adhesion on the lips
purses them despondently
as though a wilted border legume

festooned with royal imagos
gradually shrank under such attack
so moderate and in need of its spokesman
from the crazy paving to summon it
publicly and instil its virtues
in the unconscious collective able
maybe to metamorphose in the flesh
whether to transcend or sink
the submerged segments jumble
into the jammed coin slot of the drier
ready waiting to tangle
the shrunken garments which infest
those lower parts close to
the anticipated waking dream
snatched today by the sun
writhing through the glass
and curtains in a thermal aubade
administered to purge the passive
flanks of heliotrope saluting in
rank on rank led on by the left
to evaporate like haze that droops
overhead like tired pugilists
on a tour of remembrance
disliking the neat freeways
on which they speed between lights
at carefully adjusted mph
and maintained lane discipline
around the perimeter of the old town
which has been carefully restored
to the epoch of an imaginary childhood
of Easter eggs in foil
in closely guarded boxes
ready for desire unwrapped and
polished off while waiting
the nebulous crushed friables
cast off by the motor vortex
of deliquescence in the rubbery mud
which lifts like a facial mask
briefly hardened and fixed in plaster
caked on the eyes like copper
as it shrinks over the grease ready
to peel the orange off the sunset
before birds buzz ahead again

at steps through the wood and
their feathers fall like shadows or
coloured foliage in a drought
equally given for comfort or to
wear on a hat the furthest
choice is fully reconciled before
the grave is shovelled up
the wind dies down it seems
the nestlings have got round to flight
and listening expectantly for
streamers fanning through the party
air with someone's message
falling in a tangle on a lap
you bet like a novice out
for the day and slowly stifling
collapse eye to eye with an ankle
which hurries out of sight
its pair replacing it as
though sandwiched between mirrors
everything goes on diminishing like
itself like itself the recession is a
sultry war of imitation hanging
like a baggy suit of clothes
worn on the wrong occasion
suffused with sweat and flushed
around a desperate grimace or bare teeth
shining in the dark and demanding
an argument even on its last legs
trying to clamber into the ring
each foot in the way and speechless
to think of what it might do next
with just a mangled skin and no
loose ends of deceit weaving from
the cropped edges of such a brain
meant to side with its own like
an inflated stoppage which
grown into full mourning
for the child that uttered the man
on a specific genetic web
that quivered for a moment in the wake
of the earth as easing away it
left a predatory ghost to show
that exhalation fading from the glass.

Driftwood and Seacoal

These men are on their feet, not all day long, when they may be on their knees or sitting on their backsides for all I know, but characteristically and most visibly they are upright, resting or in slow motion, entire and self-contained in their activity, relentlessly static. They have overcoats and caps, and the set of their heads to their shoulders, an inflexible terseness about the neck, recurring in the way the cap flattens and spreads the skull, and the overcoat's abrupt hem straightens across a stiffness behind the knee, wraps them in mistaken identity, never close enough to make apology necessary. There is something rigid between the collar bones and the scalp, between the way the knot of the tie lies against the throat and the forehead disappears beneath the headband, as though the regularity of the features is worn like an alibi. I am not where you place me. I am going down the road leading from the council estate, I am standing on the foreshore, but who you took me for must, you now realise, be miles away from where you thought you just recognised him.

What forgiveness in renewal of such error! You return as them. Stopped short again, face to face with your type, squared off from his surroundings in which I was a passer-by, I keep forgetting that you can't be here. Forgetting the vagrancy of the moment, the distances and waiting, whatever was expected, as his figure approaches, rather flat, the weight carried down the length of the spine, short legs holding the ground beneath their feet, I am out of this place, pulled together in the passage of time. Old enough, these men must be, as if belonging anywhere was now a pointless question. Why, still there of course, as long as I can remember, looking in front of them, they're like this, wherever you are. Their memories are longer still, it shows in the hang of the coat, like a box to put things in, and the low heels of tightly knotted shoes. Years of another life, of weather in the streets and the air indoors, the hours of work, the regularity of habits, when all choices are the same, the cut of the coat, the peak of the cap, and the colour of the shoes, the size in collars, the taste in ties, the pullover and braces, determined footsteps of a steady descent, bearing it all back.

I see the difference in them, collecting from the confused after-image of wishful thinking, their presence diminished to the daily scale, going about some known business. Out for a walk will do, in these surroundings, not calling for a nod of even passing acknowledgment: people live round here. They look the same. They look out against the same earth or sea or sky, the most incommunicative of languages, speechless theatres of space, the machinery of gods. No answering back, no resonant echo, but speak for yourself. Your early history is legend, the fit of your build, the gait from the past, O never-forgotten! Those massed identities, spread one way and another, banked and scattered in new neighbourhoods. I hold them like your bearing in me, between a beacon and the showy stars, looking along the pebbles on the beach. So others in us, if, not therefore not, but also, go separately together.

The Heifer

after Carl Rakosi

From the river bank she saw the fields
with ditches round them full of water.

"The mist had gone. Where were we?"

Striped woollen dress
all morning made our order breakfast
still hungry for more toast and coffee.
The tea-urns bubbled in a corner.
We were together on stools and benches,
at snack-bar counters near the window,
in bars soon after they were open.

"Tell me. Where were we?"

We were inside
both our pasts
and our future
where our paths crossed
              in a crowded hallway
and the gas-fire of a furnished room
and an early fenland autumn
           are our memory,

where the light hardened
           into a shape
and in all directions
         earth and sky met.

We were where we have not lost
each other's separate power
as if at once
to see together . . .
the simple tenderness
of a heifer licking a post,
forever lost . . .
          forever to be lost.

Fred D'Aguiar

Mama Dot

I

Born on a sunday
in the kingdom of Ashante

Sold on monday
into slavery

Ran away on tuesday
cause she born free

Lost a foot on wednesday
when they catch she

Worked all thursday
till her head grey

Dropped on friday
where they burned she

Freed on saturday
in a new century

II

Old Mama Dot
old Mama Dot
boss a de stew-pot
she nah deal in vat
she nah bap
no style
so stop
look at Mama Dot
windin on de spot

Old Mama Dot
old Mama Dot
watch her squat
full o de nat-
-tral goodness dat
grow in de lann
she use to farm
bare hann
up evry dawn

Old Mama Dot
old Mama Dot
she nah deal wid vat-
-igan nah mek no fuss
she a deal wid duss
she swing cutlass
play big boss
lick chile rass
go to mass

Obeah Mama Dot
(her remedies)

I

I am knotted in pain.
She measures string
From navel to each nipple.

She kneads into my belly
Driving the devil
Out of my enforced fast.

II

For the fevers to subside,
I must drink the bush
Boiled to a green alluvium,

In one headback slake;
And return to bouncing around,
Side-stepping bushes for days.

III

A head-knock mushrooms
Into a bold, bald,
Softened bulb.

Her poultice filled
At the end of a rainbow—
The sun above Kilimanjaro;

The murderous vial drawn,
Till the watery mound
Is a crater in burnt ground.

IV

Our rocking-chair counsellor:
Her words untangling us
from bramble and plimpler notions

Into this sudden miles-clearing.

Mama Dot Warns Against an Easter Rising

Doan raise no kite is good friday
but is out he went out an fly it
us thinkin maybe dere wont be a breeze
strong enouf an widout any a we to hole it
fo him he'd neva manage to get it high-up
to de tree top ware de wind kissin
de ripess sweetess fruit we cawn reach
but he let out some string bit by bit
tuggin de face into de breeze
coaxin it up all de time takin a few steps back
an it did rise up bit by bit till de lang tail
din't touch de groun an we grip de palin
we head squeeze between to watch him

an trace its rise rise rise up up up in de sky
we all want to fly in like bird but can only kite
fly an he step back juss as we beginnin
to smile fo him envy him his easter risin
when bap he let out a scream leggo string
an de kite drop outta de sky like a bird
a sail down to de nex field an we runnin to him
fogetting de kite we uncle dem mek days ago
fram wood shave light as bird bone
paper tin like fedder an de tongue o kite
fo singing in de sky like a bird an de tail
fo balance string in de mout like it pullin
de longess worm an he a hole him foot
an a bawl we could a see seven inch a greenhart
gone in at de heel runnin up him leg
like a vein he groanin all de way to de haspital
on de cross-bar a bike ridden by a uncle
she not sayin a word but we hearin her
fo de ress a dat day an evry year since
doan raise no kite is good friday
an de sky was a birdless kiteless wait fo her word

Airy Hall Iconography

The Tamarind hangs its head,
stings the eyes with its breath.

The Mango traps the sun by degrees,
transforms its rays into ambrosia.

The Coconut's perfect seal lets in rain,
bends with solid milk and honey.

The Guava is its own harvest,
each seed bound in fleshy juice.

The Guinep's translucence is all yours
if you skin its lips, chew its seed for the raw.

The Stinking-toe might be lopped off a stale foot,
on the tongue it does an about-turn: myrrh.

The Paw-paw runs a feather along your nose,
you want it to stop, you want more.

The Sour-sop's veneer is the wasp
treading air at the vaulted honeycomb.

The Sapodilla ducks you twice in frankincense,
you are fished out fighting to go down a third time.

Sound Bite

The marines look vernal
in the studio lights,
caught in their nocturnal
amphibious landings.

They patrol Somalia
in monsoon rains and sun,
far from the familiar
snowstorm-flashflood-season.

They shake the bony stems
of withered hands which children,
women and shadowy men
offer saviours not friends.

The local militia
in customised armoury
dash for the interior
firing at anybody.

Laden relief convoys
will reach bandit terrain
where the too-long starved die
anyway watching grain;

the last of the children
grown accustomed to eating
the bark off sparse trees, then
absolutely nothing,

can't swallow. They perish.
Here even shallow graves
defeat the healthiest.
All the words for food have

become the stuff legends
spring from, or plain foreign,
as these helmeted men,
fresh-faced in fatigues,

tarpaulin topped trucks drop;
who hop and skip from jeeps,
fit and fat and so proud,
to feast our eyes is sweet.

Langston

I

When you studied the sea it seemed to carry
Poetry and everything you knew by reason:
A line drawn from black to white in a hurry
Called desire, formed the posturing horizon;
Another in the shape of a container or bowl
Collected light sent all those years away
To stun, flood and renew your given world;
Straight line and circle connived in a play.

Africa was in that sea, *the* Africa!
Where all the broken promises in your wake
Would be repaired and your splendid America
Righted from the leanings of past mistakes.
Langston, you can see land, smell its trouble,
Salt-breath, break the seal on that rum bottle.

II

On land, gravity kept each of us captive,
Pinned zoot suits by the lapels to the ground,
Separated colours in the strained light,
Held the tracks of two races parallel always.

In anything — but to lash out and live —
In love, we found it hard to lift our tongues;
Dragged our feet when pulled Left or shoved Right.
Gravity took the grind and wind from our waists.

At sea, I was light, lighter than vapour.
My bones, my porous bones, became feathers.
America shrunk in my wake to a slice

Of land, shrunk, until its quarrels with my race,
And all America's migratory people,
Streamed through the opal eye of a needle.

An English Sampler

A roof caves in,
        into a yard,
a yard losing
        its roof, a high
walled yard, we call
        this yard our country.

We're safe in there
        until we find
ourselves dodging
        blocks of concrete
that disintegrate
        on impact on concrete.

We can't climb those
        walls, we won't be
valiant and
        try, not in the
company of
        such young people.

So in assessment
        we praise youth,
the resilence
        thereof, the way
they are prepared
        to fall and bounce

right back up again
    while we ruminate
on possible
    pitfalls that
await us and
    befall us anyway.

To youth for showing
    how to walk away
from the knock on
    effect of the
knock on the head
    or to the heart

or broken bones.
    This is England,
though it could be
    anywhere. We are
not herders but
    teachers. We mend

the bones and soothe
    the broken heads,
tell those big hearts
    the hurt will lessen.
The roof we crossed
    to get this far

threatened to cave
    in under us
even as we crawled
    along shadows
judged to be steel
    rafters, in pairs,

scraping our bellies,
    hands and knees on
anti-climb paint
    and praying that
those kids, our kids
    won't see us now.

Ken Edwards

Five Nocturnes, after Derek Jarman

1

About this time streetlamps flicker up like
Work of art in an age of mechanical reproduction,
Pink pin pricks slowly flower pink to gold glare.
All of a sudden Baby starts to speak fluent german,
A man & his dog become shadow of a man & his dog
Spontaneously everything is terrifically brilliant.
Each evening takes a photograph each evening
Becomes lighter; worm of power grows.

Gold burns in lightbulb egg or golden apple
Burns in satin now that's ruined your day.
Very important lots of money
No information at all flowers bloom sodium
Fuels brilliant sunsets seen behind protective glass.
Bang bang shoot shoot in every art gallery.

2

An art of definition — is this
— surface of hand on surface (boundary)
Of glass? or is it "I intend to jump
Off this ledge & get happy"?

Writing unwrites itself into
Chance encounters configurations
That are politically indeterminate like rubber
Ball trajectories in a confined

Space; but an art of definition; at what
Point does the ink itself begin to
Speak what does it say

Why want to make time stand still?
Between lightbulb & the idea of lightbulb
Falls the shadow.

3
This juxtaposition of events without
Perspective: chinese mat, magazines, ash-tray,
Concord sonata 1st american in space.
On a glass table the objects, held
By the circle that bounds them,
Struggle to break free of the authoritarian
Figure, with its connotation
Of repeating, & the idea of a centre.

So you keep hanging onto the appearances
How they might be saved by epicycle
Upon epicycle in the comforting dark
When sodium flare reveals those orbits
Twin focussed, not as they might be,
Ineluctably tousled as they are.

4
De—um majorettes
                              Doin' mah writin'
Clear light evening
                              Goes down slowly

Not finished—not yet
Who is responsible for these
Black silhouettes
A magic zone a protected zone

Became the laziest 8th king
2 goats pandas crabs & a friesian bull
What's the connection

Buy emphasizers, cow gum, album for art work
New FT index
Will blow your mind

5
Night falls on single vision zombies everywhere
O that lonely Feb. moon in a clear sky
Occasionally perceived between the flats is it
(a) mythopoeic construct (b) collage?

If there's an answer there must be a
Question (Gertrude Stein). Write the essentials only.
Moonlight on wilting
                             Spider plant, make
Shadows
                     Gone
Whirling through stages of a spiral blood game

Nights in the city. so pretty. so
Slovenly, lovely. all of us here
Breathing out. breathing in. breathing out

Good Science

The drill sergeants break up the only road we've got
The angry woman rings it starts to rain
I state my case on the basis of need
You shoot it down on the basis of want

This week has given me a new grasp of particle physics
You see how the glands in your throat do swell
So profitability extends to the Silurian layers
The Dow is up the unit starts to break down

A light plane trails red fly north-west orient
I've managed to lie down on the floor just once
The embarrassment factor peaked now & again
Neoclassicism was a reaction to this "dangerous future"

My legs started to shake uncontrollably
They are not objects but networks of relationships
She was smoking & talking for the first time
A threequarter century rhythm punctuates diurnal priorities

Morosely a pearly king & queen get off the train
A gunshot spoils the tidal rhythm
Take away the underlying phrase-length & improvisation remains
Does fortune play the strumpet with me now?

It was a projection outward of active perception
It was my muscles starting to open up
Maybe get sunflowers for the sunny wall
Her voice is a beautiful city that doesn't exist

We spent a most pleasant evening thank you
Liberated from the bar-line the grid-lit slabs reverberate
I tend to dissolve into the usual
You couldn't take more than an hour so left

After a heavy day the book was no more than adequately clear
The pound started trembly the board sent the dollar down
Now there's no objective way of measuring space
So the room moves into & out of phase with my conception

The elephant house is blinded with plywood
It contains the ghosts that language doesn't need
I could have gone to the music but didn't feel like it
You could have had salt beef rice & mixed pickle

Small children lay multicoloured hoops on the new tarmac
Contrast the yellow-grey gloom & the white glare
Extended intervals are occurring
It pervades my whole life at the moment

I bought a book on the subject & immediately felt guilty
They stayed in bed arbitrarily distanced
The big building is full of really crazy people
The man is 22 & has 2 tattoos

She cites brachiation as the original divergence
Scored for 6 bass clarinets & 6 contrabass clarinets
You dovetail neatly into the above stuff
I wake up I open the refrigerator I don't know where I am

Lexically

soaked into a p Aste fine breaker slant
faking its Beat yet more for dollar use
the shore's a Chieving
Dies labels eyes to stare
breeding into an Error
the Flame & terror
the hero's meaner langua Ge
wild purrs cat in the Home
and all of th Is most fake too
right brain sizzles: wince Jelly: face of brine described
a tent of bile a huger whis Ky
"self-ref Lexive"
the Man did the breath in the voice
i Nto girl or brick or large
infusion Of derivation
sho P sales flattening off
earth Quakes
a bongo soft in some wan d Rizzle drum offers pity
was all that could be Sought
on a la Te november afternoon
all asia dreams yo U
gender radar! View not imagine
circle the World or forfeit
towards e Xile any directory
i stole the bab Y
gained a mellow darling ha Zard learning

Provisionally

Launch into writing and you launch into the unnamed future, with language
as a cutting edge. The problem: how to negotiate the forming events without
postural collapse of the psyche, a regression this side of painful learning. I crawl
across the floor, but I do not become a baby again. The "point" of the activity?
Is it to regain animal grace, or to forfeit innocence properly and so get happy in
an awareness welter?

Clouds gather in the morning above a city's multiple configurations; they precipitate rain as the day grows older; then began to disperse, giving way to patches of blue sky and sunshine striking off the wet tarmac. Towards evening, the waning sunlight fills a window, clarifying every smear and speck. A difference of universes, shop-soiled against the resonance. Interest abates till a tall type hazes, stops ales flattening. Off-chances of cumulus gladly sit by the pall on precipices. Transitive bullets abate. It's fear (of being) (in the world) that brings disease to the body that should be haunted by poetry and made translucent by its inner combustion. Perception has become learning, and the next moment begins here.

Unconsciously

Drum heartbeat is present
Matches breathing fire
Enriching life
Burning sets here
A laser beam
To continue transforming
The simultaneous birth
Inspires the powerful
Hounded with doctorates
He walks right into the room
Accompanied by jumps
Valves create a voice
Deeply involved in quality
Astound the exploding
Noble & difficult
Crisp & solid
Call it a feeling
In the heart of imagination

An external behaviour
Feels that violation
With events of quality that
Dissolve in that sense
Now opens our ears
Things in the world
Matrix of disaffection
Institutions that offend us
Structuring the nuclear
Persons there beyond
Want them to be here
For you now specifically
Food we want to know
Drain that we don't go down
You're making a choice
Eating all that underlies
Action of a type
Spirit of their own

Peter Finch

Scaring Hens

kid kid kid kootje
kid kid kid kootje
kootje
        kutch
kootjie
        kutch kutch
kootjie
good-chick
good good
good-chick
good good good
good-chick
ha cudies, kud-dids, cudies, cuddles,
cud-ducks, kud-chuck, diddles, doddles,
cuddles, gidi-gidi cuddles,
good good, gidi-gidi,
gidi gidi, gud gud,
gwd gwd
good good
        good good
good
CUT CHICK CUT CHICKS
KWIT KWIT
CUT GOOTCH
GOOTCH CUTCH CUT CUT
gootch gootch cut coo
cwtch (goots)
gwsh
        jee cootch coo
coo coo cootch
        cwtsh cwtsh cwtsh
cwtsh cwtsh cwtsh
wheeeeeeeeeeeeeeeeee
wishsh got got
whist got cot cot

cot got cot cot
cot cot got cot
KWIT CUT CHICK
KWIT
goodi
goodi goodi goodi
goodi goodi goodi
goodi goodi goodi
goodi goodi goodi
goodi goodi goodi
goodi goodi
good.

Source: *Animal Call Words — David Thomas OBE*

Reds in the Bed

chair and bed red
a red chair and bed
chair and bed red
a red bed and a chair
a red chair bed
and a bed chair red
chair red and a bear
a bear chair and a red bed
a rare bear and a red bear
a red rare bare bear
bare chair red head bear
bare chair head bear
red bare red chair red hair
red hair red hair red hair
red hair red hair red hair
red air red air red air
red bear and bed chair
chair bear and an air bed
air bear and a chair bed
red bed and a red bed
red bear and an air bed
rare bed and an air bare
air bare red head in an air bed
red head in an air bed

red head on an air bed
red head in an air bed

Source: *Welsh Phonology*

Marks The English Left On The Map

shake hole
shake hole
shake hole
shake hole
sheepfold
dismantled tramway waterfall
waterfall waterfall pan
area of quarry (dis)
glass cairn wire bank
swallow shake
mine all mine (bdy)
sheepfold pothole

[OS Brecon Beacons Central Area Copyright The Crown]

How Callum Innes Paints

I can't solve this
I am too young

limit limit confused

I turn away among ambitions
and limitations ss edit the

How the hell can I ever make
another one

limit the pure sufficient ity

I know lim I know lim I know how
I know lim I know the purity

I can't rely
I know the mythology

sufficient process not lim not purity
I know how the process not the
limit the field the state

ambition turnaway

unsolvable

look anyway

Why Do You Want To Be English?

You can't do English much
a lot of them
really don't have much to do with English
I'm English they are going to steal my cattle

Does doing an English
overlaid with a false English
mean you are not British
English is a straw dog, a real dilemma

I am interested in English as one blossom
one hundred percent English free of guilt
not my ancestors ran the Roman Empire

The choice:
Cambridge English
Elgar
Hardy
English Bengali like the remnants of Bosnia
I could go on

English disjuncture like a blind stick
please speak clearly after the long tone
archipelago consensus   no longer a land mass
do not write anything down

Allen Fisher

African Boog

Went dicing on my bike
>Disappearance

>Meaning given by timbre

>Relational invariants from a flux

>She lives in advance of her days

>>Speed

Rooks carry aubergines over Tulse Hill station
>He hung an 18 foot blackboard in the garden

>In all the beautiful continuity of hope

>>The innocent

She crossed Hillside Road with her sun lamp
>Thought confused by recall

>A car in flames

>>IN the climate

>Distress of need

>Moments when the go different two-beat series

>These are birds is an illusion

>>Confront

>Down the escalator that ascends

>Constitutents of multiplicity unaffected by transformation

>Pauses, and, introspections

>>Their own terror

From his mouth produced a net curtain the length of his body
>'Surrendered myself to magic, that is physics.'

>Watching myself burning from a distance

>>Spectacle it unleashes

>Authority, perfection, oppression

>Moments when series go different the two-beat

>Improvises from consistent memory

>>Violent in itself

>Her attitude's beyond music called indirection

>Configurational relativity, the sound of language

Dissing on my skate board
>>Population

>Your patience is exhausted with someone

'To catch a fly on the moon'
The default of the garden's charm
    Each other
Hooks vary auburn jeans overt until fashion
    Discontinuous strata, unsteady sediments
    Closes behind her the gate of childishness
        Always ends up
All the oranges, but one, turned blue
    Tripped up by details
    Down Electric Avenue in a garbage press
        In future war
    Overlapping fourths with thirds
    Essential and accidental property.
    The sound of the heard and the played
        With dirty hands
    'How to count the stars while riding a bike'
    Moments when go different the two-beat series
    There are birds singing
        Deterrence
    Cycling into seeds and mud
    Relativity on the flip of invariance.
Autonomous order disorder
        Truly violent
    Juxtapose time a-cross-rhythm
    Your forehead blur-laps beneath mustard field
    Two moments when the two-beat series coincide
        Only the turn
    A metal box in flames
    Constructed proof for consistency
    In perpetual *leans* accelerates
        Against the military
    Fools about contemporary with falling
    Topological correspondences unfold similar linguistics together.
    Extemporise from inventive memory
        Superversive
    The *shapes* of the figures 2 and 3 make music
    Loved to dance
    She enters the enchanted garden
        Because insoluble
    At the velocity of milk in a vacuum flask
    The rough edges, the false starts.
    Just pumping up my tyres
        The spectacular

In opening amazement a tulip stretched beyond return
A misdirected intensity of discovery itself
That this isn't universal experience
      Simulation
She's lost in a mode with a fun loop
      Stratigraphical completeness sifted in differences
Expectations may be high
      And appear suddenly
Foam, issued-out produce, a certain learning commodity
      Spans far longer than experience
Just warming the pot
      Terrorists, public opinion
A direct hit on the waste basket
Undecidable
In a purple lean-to, accumulates
      System which
Walking down the drain and laughing
Contextual and stylistic alteration
Buckled beneath a fruit stall crying
      The stupidity
Counterpoint reduced to fracture two and three beats
'Tables, chairs, and beer mugs'
Spontaneity from electro-chemical decision
      To exterminate joy
Juxtapose pitch notes melody
Disappears in bluebells   wood-light   may.
Moments when the two-beat series go different
      Actuality can be the meant
Absorb myself by watching
'He looked so *innocent*'
Crouched in a doorway mumbling
      To palm all that is reported
Juxtapose harmony-notes vertically chords
Every turn within change;   joy and worry
Just ratatouille on the gas
      Innocence
Brixton market frequent, Brixton market full music
At odds with results from everyday
Just imagining pleasure
      MAKES all the variables
Tempered by the moon on his shoulders
Instead of feedback through the eye as a basis.
Perhaps an uncommon or personal experience

A minimally real event
Orangutans guessed, but one yearned it was true
　　Few study deposits for as long as a decade
　　Its shades slow with promise
　　　Flashing
The chair left through the window
　　The proposition without deduction from other propositions
　　Play drum with the drums being heard
　　　In a maximal echo chamber
　　Two moments when series coincide the two-beat
　　'The laws of nature's independence from the choice of mollusc.'
　　Tigers are in cages, tigers are in cages
　　　The contradiction in situ
　　The mud of perfection
　　Relations that have a finite ideal
　　Just come in
　　　Does utopia
　　With joy and fear small thoughts at large
　　The process being followed conceptual and executive together
　　Skyline in the window
　　　Patterns how many years
　　A civilisation based on dancing
　　Assumptions on visual evidence reduced to syntax
　　A mix of two-beat moments invigorates texture
　　　To open for measuring time
　　Flames
　　This volume determined by the size of needle
　　Just smiling as you
　　　The personal alters consciousness
　　Shape of your eyes' dilations condense brights
　　The particulars of each plant heightened by common structures.
　　Absorbing the memories chemically
　　　Changes
　　Two moments two-beat series coincide when the
　　Stars detail variability shows an average everywhere the same
　　Horizon into the window, the siren
　　　Initiates
　　Older parallels and pseudo-parallels overlap
　　'Tomorrow we went to the forest'
　　Just playing in the mud
　　　To think about a problem publicly
　　Shone from a helicopter onto a tulip

The rug rolled away
More often than not reprevented
    Political to value slowness
At viscosity of spilt ink vacant tasks
Stratas record positive deposits, but what else happened?
Blowing metal into tumblers of cells
    Had taken the possible
JUST ICE
Immediacy at the thresholds structures activity, that is perceptions
From the balcony over the tulips, the church
    The society made by men
Juxtapose timbre vibrato to patterns vertically and horizontally
Opens a glow-out red jacket in a crowd.
Asleep in a hammock, accelerates
    Dance collaged into reel
Conversation and your breath bell
'It happened that I found myself tomorrow'
Four playing cards on a box in a crowd
    Implosive order abolishes
A language based on tone and timbre
'No one will drive us out of this paradise'
Seduction turns to exploitation
    System of repression
Her stare reft thought in a winder
Span's illusion independent of the probable.
Stolen wallets on a bread crate in a crowd
    The order of transgression
Indiginer and invader overlap
'It was tomorrow'
Space toys on a pavement in a crowd
    The old bacteria of law and cultured intrusion
Speech patterned horizontally and vertically
'Ya! Ya! Ya!'
Or enchantment becomes repression
    Value, meaning, determination
Asbestos beauty snapped in a rain storm
Reality a requirement for perfection
The sound of memory-played with memory-being-absorbed.
    Excess of rarity
Two moments series coincide when the two-beat
Without limits, the universe of these beings is finite.
A street in havoc, exasperates authority

Law, point of view, evidence
Lifts from a spring board into cloud
'Temporal separation a tenacious illusion'
Every turn of the path seductions
Entrenching the desires of others
As best as you can rapped from the brain bourne
Jump on bike, figure of eight around rose beds, to the
blackboard.

Birdland

1   An image of the Engineer's model
    shudders in a basement
    as sand stabilisers are loaded.
    The left arm bright gold, the ears glow green.
    Out of its head energy spatialises
    overlappings of spiralic fields.
    A figure appears to attempt flight,
    it may have wings, yet held to the floor
    accelerates towards an openness through liberation
    of its partner, unseen from the pit entrance.
    Is it male? What is there to say
    concerning child birth?
    Its presence takes place
    between table and pasture, at this moment
    takes space between road and underground river:
    it is named jouissance:
    The arrival.
    It brings experience of radical separation of self,
    like child birth, produces an object of love.

2   In the morning television I carry
    a cylinder of heat in my embrace
    down a garden path labelled by the placing of stones,
    Hey Bellman, someone shouts,
    puts a match to a felled lime
    lengthways in the walkway
    with meanderings of drama
    thought I was moving forward
    lost ground

in mistakes, with grinding gaps in what I know about
fidelities or reproduction. By chance, it seemed,
back to the path I had opened
Its trace visible in footmarks and
potential infinity to an unknown fold.
On certain days, this morning is an example,
I remove my helmet cross the path
with a slight intoxication
to check the lime has been properly extinguished.

Endless destruction
makes Brixton
Call it the coexistence of prohibitions and
their transgression
Call it carnival and spell out jouissance and horror,
a nexus of life and description, the child's
game and dream plus discourse and spectacle.
On the edge
of death High Road, the Busker
starts up a reel, it begins as dance interlaced
with anger. I guess at the ridiculous partners
that perform. The busker dances with
her saxophone
'Ideas of Good and Evil' are subsumed into this nexus,
production knots and
unknots paranoia
Blake stands his ground
on the Common asks, Are
    Her knees and elbows only
       glewed together.

3   A woman came down the walkway
    lost in transport
    exploded her language at a kid
    with a stick
    restrained by another who breaks
    the rod across his leg,
    We've had enough, got it! We've had enough!
    One hour later someone has dragged
    a felled lime onto the walkway
    Its leaves make a green path

A pack of dogs surround this, yelp
out of phase. Down the High Road
a new siren on a police weapon
fills the walkway
It leaves a burnt fizz overhead
grooves the mud plane on the roof.
Next door fits an extension to his aerial
changes tone of CB interference
in loudspeakers makes audible
amplified pulses from a geranium
in a Faraday cage. A poster snaps the letterbox.
Come to Paradise in Brixton's Coldharbour.

4   Beneath helicopters
Brixton abandoned
challenges the closure of meaning
so far removed, nothing will have taken place but the place,
flattened housing for ecological reasons,
fuses with a beyond, a successive clashes in
formations, memories of bodily contact, but
warmth and nourishment do not underlie the air.
The Mathematician
gets on the subway in a pinstriped
with a microchip blackboard. A spotted handkerchief
matches his tie. On the back of his head someone
has singed a domino it
matches his ear rings. As he starts to leave
his accounts, he pulls the arms from his jacket,
sets them alight.
The effect is laughter,
an imprint of an archaic moment, a threshold of
spatiality as well as sublimation.
Suddenly a path clears Sleep relates the squeezed
State to a lack of community He leans
towards me, Last night, he insists,
I had a strange dream.

5   The imaginary takes over from laughter,
it is a joy without words, a riant spaciousness
become temporal.
The demonstrative points to an enunciation,
it is a complex shifter straddling the fold of

naming it, and the autonomy of the subject.
Wearing four tones of grey soap I
read photocopied pages on lighting effects,
the Mathematician battery-shaves and makes
notes on squeezed light using a notation
echoed by remnants of beard clung to hydrogen
on his trousers. Subjection to meaning gets
replaced with morphology. I become a mere
phenomenal actualisation moved through a burning gap.
The irrational State insists on control.

from *Stepping Out*

Stepping Out: I

  δ Being in earnest
 ←↓ The emergence of post-transformation
   Bloom in the plain acoustic
←↓→ Derive explicit transformations
   Towards reliance on words that reveal
   Sheer delicacy colours textures of transparency
   Rhythm pervades of dotted crotchet and quaver
   Involuntary contractions discharge excitation
   To search the requirements of responsive commitment
↑↓∞~ A short rest itself prolonged.

Progressions of Spacetime: I

Today a brown duck with a green head
Blue shoes a pink umbrella
Love of the rule which collects the emotion
Rain puddles rain light rain drain steam
Observation and modulation to say I love you
Understand the seen between the eyes and the held
Spacetime phased inside watcher and, the tendency
 interpret literally
The function to enrich the emotions, the eyes, the fingers

Colour and substance contribute as megaphone
Take into account the situation created by production.

Rims of Distinction: I

Dynamic marking cuts through the fill-up
A spin of shifts telescoped
A bounce of shapes and procedures
Recur at an analytical level
Taking away glistening surfaces
Mirror canon matched by translucence
The simplicity of affection
Searching superimposed planes
What counts unexpected.

Stepping Out: 2

       Deliberation and flow blend
←↓ The emergent post-transformation
       Molecular common to utterance
←↓→ Explicit derivations
       Thankfully spacetime becoming discontinuous
       Waves of dense clusters
       Become more deliberate than personality
       The smallest detail relates functionally to design
       To share the conviction that limits can be overstepped.

The "universal symbols" in the margins refer to arm/hand movements during reading performance:
← from the body horizontally
→ to the body horizontally
↑ rising
↓ falling
δ flow motion from the body
∞~ infinity gesture in waves

from *Emergent Manner*

Machynlleth

Virtually whole they perceive it and name it *Anagallis tenella*
Explicitly fragment fray receive them as they drop into stellar peat and sigh
Continual recognition and repeated examples at every creeping stem
Manual connotation end pleated river stream tender and delicate
A process of *structuring*, a process of conservation
An express for elating a constellation in exquisite bells
No mere collection of elements, no mere random effect
Shot fear collage for instruments of chrome and jet microscopes
Legalities of properties the stewardship from stalls
Legality of prophecies, a ship of fools guess the next event
Preserved interplay of laws guarantee pimpernel in the damp
Reserved inner stray corse in the stank of the wind pool
Wholeness transformation, self-regulation, insulated light
Bold necessity explores self undulates the first tick of summer.

The Diary Theme

Correlation which unites the human condition
Portrayal switch rights an extended rendition of Spenser
A bunch of 'passionified' carrots to make the eyes gleam
Crunch of fashioned scare crows to exercise spleen and buzz off
How production of perception itself leads inner story
Now reduction of receipt begins to self bore me
Encourages narrativity and prevention's dream state roar
Until copy parades convention, demonstrates to the poor their waste away
How evolution to simulate promotes extinction
Now revolution to emulate derives from distinction downloaded
Led to consciousness with microchip implant
Shed proprioception and gave decision to aunt sally the message
Ideas of consciousness left to minimal morals
Identity of proprioception with social quarrels and their allegorical forms.

Murder One

The processes activities break drop and disappear
The crocuses practicate skates spear the mist
Multiple-intersecting plateaux pierces thought cluster
Terrible invective plateaux where the knowns muster mistake
Rhizomic electro-bio-chemistry flakes the proceed
Rise direct proto-metonymy burns the need to see this
Consequent chreods mitigate against change
Contributes desire to gain a range and shake it off
Complex analyses, described rhetorically from a podium
Raw sex banalities derived rheology spasm then hold
Theories of proprioception en route to loneliness
Periodic consciousness rapidly prone to field
Images, recurrences, memory, before tape stretches
Mazes, crucibles, metaphor enough fetches to stave off common sense.

The Ditchley Portrait

That that mind perceives how to fly alone
Trap at grind receives bite into flesh and bone as a need
Establishes *verum factum* or the true and made
Crashes verse fact momentum converts the staid into momenergy
Without knowing superimposed terms without crack in the esteem
Inner crowing exposed the pure and pristine false consciousness
Shape of entities one and the same in the neck-clamped sublime
Gravity before expansion done with again in a spacetime short of emotion
Meaningful as they find a within and levitate into air
Wearing full cake bind before now and there as the clouds lift the Ditchley portrait
Poetic metaphysical and physical scan of multiple horizons
Poetic ecstatic and actual blast of surprising's eventual banality.
That humankind constructs myths only to summarise
When crystal dilates message to distinguish shape from size at lift off.

Roy Fisher

from *The Cut Pages*

He paints words with the past

Give us something, give us something

If I do, you'll regret it

The defective mirror plucks at a glove. It is passing, it is passing the mirror. The mirror's defect is to pluck what slips

Tumbled. Strewn. Built. Grown. Allowed

I was going to say it but I won't. You can be going to say yours. I was going to say it because I knew it

Click

The second day. Was that the first?

Hats are in evidence, but precious little else. I mean the men aren't

Spread. Examine the spread and report back to spread-head

                                        Coaling at intervals along the line

Yes, forming into lines, little clusters of lines, little directional urgencies of line-clusters, unexpected accelerations of urgencies

Yawning into urgencies unprepared

Slats and shades, heads and shoulders, afternoons look at afternoons

Lengthening, passing over, surfacing over. You're not recoverable. Take only what you need. Why travel heavy if you can travel light?

Stop this one. My shoe. No, it's gone

Spread. By close proliferation so instantaneous, no more than a tight rustle, it seemed pre-existent. Nothing could move. Nothing should want to

Three smiles

Three smiles from the same

Three smiles from different people

All footways lead up from this bollard

Sliver

Edge-on presenting itself. And a conspiracy to stop a person getting a clear idea of where his various limbs are; in what and with what mobility

Yes, the spirit of it all

They're on the run, scurrying past to the edge of town, and back again. We're not. It's their turn, whoever they are

Don't say *engulf*

Cross marked on the pane, cut into the glass. Small shining scratches

The Burning Graves at Netherton

This is a hill that holds the church up.

This is a hill that burned
part of itself away:

down in the coal measures
a slow smoulder

breaking out idly at last
high on the slope

in patches
among the churchyard avenues.

Netherton church lifts up
out of the falling land below Dudley;

on its clean promontory
you see it from far off.

Not burning. The fire
never raged, nor did the graves flame
even by night, the old
Black Country vision of
hell-furnaces.

A lazy dessication. The soil first
parched, turned into sand, buckled
and sagged and split. In places
it would gape a bit, with soot
where the smoke came curling out.

And the gravestones
keeled, slid out of line,
lifted a corner, lost
a slab, surrendered
their design; caved
in. They hung their grasses
down into the smoke.

Strange graves in any case;
some of them edged
with brick, even with glazed white
urinal brick, bevelled
at the corners; glass
covers askew
on faded green and purple
plastic diadems of flowers.

Patchy collapses, unsafe ground.
No cataclysm. Rather
a loss of face, a great
untidiness and shame;

Silence. Absence. Fire.

Over the hill, in the lee,

differently troubled,
a small raw council estate
grown old. Red brick
flaky, unpointed,
the same green grass uncut
before each house.
Few people, some boarded windows,
flat cracked concrete roadways
curving round, and a purpose-built
shop like a battered command-post.
All speaking that circumstance
of prison or institution
where food and excrement are close
company. Concrete, glazed brick
for limits. A wooded hill
at its back.

Silence. Absence. Fire.

Rules and Ranges for Ian Tyson

Horizons release skies.

A huge wall has a man's shoulder. In the only representation we have it is mottled with a rash and distorted overall, seen through gelatine.

The Thames with its waterfronts; a fabric with a Japanese Anemone design. They intersect at Chaos.

The force of darkness is hard, rigid, incapable of motion either within its own form or by way of evasion. All the same, it is very difficult to find.

The experience of a wind, as if it were a photogravure made of dots. To be vastly magnified.

To walk along two adjacent sides of a building at once, as of right.

After a fair number of years the distasteful aspects of the whole business become inescapable. Our frustrations will die with us, their particular qualities unsuspected. Or we can make the concrete we're staring at start talking back.

Watch the intelligence as it swallows appearances. Half the left side, a set of tones, a dimension or two. Never the whole thing at once. But we shouldn't need to comfort ourselves with thoughts like this.

Under the new system some bricks will still be made without radio receivers or photo-electric elements. No potential for colour-change, light-emission, variation of density—just pure, solid bricks. They'll be special.

A terror ruffling the grass far off, and passing without coming near. Between that place and this the grass is a continuous stretch with no intervening features.

Under the new football rules the goals will be set, not facing each other down a rectangle but at the centres of adjoining sides of a square pitch, and the teams will be arranged for attack and defence accordingly. Some minor changes in rules are bound to be necessary, but there will also be rich variations in styles of play.

Darkness fell, surrounding and separating the hollow breves. They howled and shone all night.

Richard II

The wiring appears to be five years old
and is in satisfactory condition.
The insulation resistance is zero.
This reading would be accounted for by the very damp condition of the building.
If you come up the stairs on the left side you will see
A band of dense cumulus massed on the banister.
Whatever you do, do not touch the clouds.
Forever again before after and always

In the light of the quiet night and the dark of the quiet noon
I awoke by a day side and I walked in time's room.
To the end of the long wall and the back of the straight floor
I stepped with my years' clutch and the dark of my days' doom.

For the sight of the deep sad and the swell of the short bright
Bid me flee waste of the time web and the long hand
On a life's weft and the grey warp in the year's cloak
For a long shade laps a short stand.

The terms left right front and rear are used
as if one is standing outside the building
facing the front elevation.
Specialists are carrying mirrors to the bedroom.
They are stacked beneath the window three foot deep.
Whatever you do, do not look in the mirror.
Again before forever after and always

The step to and the step back from the still glass in the long wall
Flung the glance wide from the old field and the brown scene.
And the glance broke at the pale horse on the glass turf
While the door swung where the window should have been.

With the ghosts gone and the wall as flat as the clock's tick
With a blood stopped and a bone still I squeezed glue from my cold glove

And I turned back to my smashed self and the few looks pierced my own doll
From the back-lash of the time brick and the last wall of an old love.

In the joinery timbers there is new infestation
And a damp-proof course is urgently needed.
Say a few prayers to the copper wire.
Technicians are placing flowers in the guttering
They are welding the roof to a patch of sky
Whatever you do, do not climb on the roof.
Before forever after again and always.

limpid eyelid

Lemon and Rosemary

for Catherine Cullen

Nobody. I, myself.
Shooting live subjects in pictures sung with imagination and wrung with truth.
Dean knew it was blackmail.

Though my deserted frying pans lie around me
I do not want to make it cohere.
Hung up to dry for fishing lines on the side of grey wharf of Lethe.
Old, we love each other and know more.

Is this a chisel that I see before me.
If so I want to hack my name on the bedroom door.

A star shines on the hour of our meeting:
Lucifer, son of morning. And
Thanks for your lighter I have forgotten the matches.

O, why do I hate doctors so?
There was a time some years ago . . .
But do dial one o o o o

On the best battle fields
No dead bodies

TM

gamebagkeeper dealt detachable breath
of the heaven and air of the waters
the earths of stones of formed stones
of plants
of Brutes of men
and women of arts of antiquities
bounce back field trip
to concrete roads mangled crash barrier economy
as falcon feather penned
cruising runover prey
I
quote
from
plot

tribulation sound surface verification
inaudible blood spillage a scrawl on walls
bled through body
oration swallowed to electric music
spiritualised belly anger
nirvana of the city levellers
desire acts at the next labyrinth
up your windows
come two
at
a sky burial

we live a block away
raised eyebrows
does it come from the edge
bank collapsed rubble charged mindheartache
state of shock   shines leatherjacket skin
an inflation dissolves to work all rules
thieves unworthy we are beautiful

twins of centre mainstream brochure blues
string-laden
sound by this light predicting magic hands
tombstone babies read to from lead pages
eyes influenced water deeply into opacity of
clouds gathering
sing to a mugshot profile of moon cast over bridge
wharf the water mud from its bed bottom
river swells
notions of raising above the common level
ran i between them against the trees ringed by
sediment scars
lost at the roots
as cavern walls seen from within culture of mould
i am a wall comparison you noted spirit
skylarking behind symbols drum to lever a whisper
calling just another polysyllabic echo
voice through water walks
to bull work
and repeats a whole hexameter verse
but not so strong as woodstock
a fowling scene in wood-cut
save ourselves curve cuckoo

we ditched

forget your lines burnt out
fundamentalist guide to getting cracked
crossing wonder border
man your man
contraband passed by neo-clans
what fitting shelves and steel merges into wet
moss
a channel wind gloss
frying pan vista
take up the heat floods sun on screen
a mumble appropriates

system at the cinema
a class spectrum projection
hover three screens as large birds only seen in a
dream

told with savannah breath
of a lost soundtrack fading

writing   moored
enter log
rumble powered
across age

from *Dents*

baseline pressure
oblige the bound
of shadows
taking the window
seek light
that lampe in a sound
or the light of-some-body
under the object
ray other shadows
seen on the floores
same centre the place
saying of the shadow a torch
and search or to speak beacon
which line from hollow
taken on foot
flexible volume
in dance in
darkening clouds
incidentally
connecticut
look space in the eye

Harry Gilonis

Song 9

for Ian Pace

and their hands, the way
they hold their hands,
pianists I mean, in
the pauses, poised, held,
in a way thought
could only default,
and still, still as a leaf
curled as it dried,
or a crab's shell
upright on shingle

an answer to Herrick

for Trevor Joyce

men turn to rocks
& rivers

when sick
of other men

more obdurate
than rock

when that
is undesirable

more yielding
than water

when that
is no virtue

orange birch bolete (*Leccinum versipelle*)
from *Forty Fungi*

hunting with
stomachs,
with eyes

at the margins
of aspen
& grassland

speckled stipes
tufted, tubes
mouse-grey;

under the fell
where the short-
eared owls

weren't, you
were,
but fly-et!

Song for Annie

follow the clews
and you will arrive at
something

we are not isolate, moving
without purpose
but "in the world;
for use, therefore . . . worthwhile"

         *

light through clouds
on the high hills
is not there
for or from our naming
but
will let us near

*

at the heart of it all
a quiet

*

a pause in the talk, a
caesura in the love-making
and
my eye scans feet
body rests

the act of poetry,
not the art

*

and my song: take care, o
                <u>take</u>
                care

Jonathan Griffin

Venerating Senses Save Us

Despair has prevented praise, but praise shall rise again
    beyond despair I will praise here and now

the ordered tones and intervals of the raindrops—how
        each drop belongs
    to one of the numbered magnitudes (double the last
    and half the next, with none between)

    and praise the reason: droplets descending spin
        some clockwise others widdershins
which opposite revolving   draws together pairs
of drops   but only the equal, which sink at the same pace.
So the liquid lapse is a fabric—the bricks of the rain build
    the First Temple the portal rainbows, one
        for each lifted-up gaze.

        And let no despair
          stop
      praise for the human ear
      staker of music—picking
out of the welter of waves   octaves and simple scales
    and from them forming a pride of rainbows
glancing.
      Man—ear—word
      that builds with the bricks of the
rain!
    Angels tread that ladder, dancing

        *

    Rough hexagons are a common
      result of stresses meeting—
      each of the workers swells
      his clamped cell
          until
—geometry of jostling—the wax froth sets.

Pappas of Alexandria, though, believed that the bees chose
                              the hexagonal cell   knowing
         this would enclose most honey in least wax,
                  and desert Basil (forgetting the stings)
         imagined that the bees were monks and wise.
         Man put beauty into honeycombs,
         religious love gave to the bees its wisdom.

         In a froth / in a honeycomb / in a mind
                  the outer cells' outward surfaces
                  curve   smoothly—the inter-faces
                         pack, polyhedral, pointed.
                  O seeking senses, locking logic,
                  pressing cells pressed to prisms
                         to make a mind!   what light
                  shall pierce your dark, suffuse your night?
                  what light is bright for you to break
         to splinter into splendour as you eat
         to drink its singleness only to pour
                  (shattered yet whole and though caught pure)
                  out through crystal simplicity
                  spectra true to complexities?

                                        *

                  Angels prefer, for all their wings,
                  the ladder—the bright bridge that springs
                              more soaring from
                              a human dream.
         Feet   than fanning feathers far more light
                         descending! fleet
                  flames of pentecostal feet
                  upon the risen silver rungs
         between a hushed soul and the singing height!

         Chaldean seekers constellated the stars—
         which our undoing doubt
                              shows as one cosmic rout . . .
                  Age of reverence without
                  faith—not praying, to praise.

                                        JONATHAN GRIFFIN   89

Dextrorse and sinistrorse torsion—weaned and grave
the proportional drops calling their equals as they fall—
            affinities of turning love—
the seven terraces, the spectrum, hang in every speck
            gardens beckoning . . .
                                    O take—
                        quick!—your babylon turn,
glad—though the fall be faster the splash at the end little
higher—
to have reflected more of the primal light returning:
                        refracted it to kind fire.
            Bricks like eyes   that eyes on Earth may make
                        suddenly burn—
courses of colour on high   the thin arch crossing the sky

                        Make the final silence
                        a silence after music

                                    1956/1977

One's Country

The universe is large: to be eccentric
is to be nothing.   It is not   worth
speaking of. (Bronk)
                        Something is worth
the speech of us eccentrics: namely, Earth.

To be Earth patriots
                        is to become not nothing,
Earth being of the Universe not the centre
                        but
                                    the sense

The Emperor

. . . shivering
Man most naked
of us all . . .   George Oppen

Yes
        since Man has
no manproof clothing

                    the weather
which will kill him is
                his

Night Sky Hiss

Secreted by long minds, antenna shell—
        giant ear-trumpet ear-to-sky
            awash with   the highest
sea's   inviolable surf-soft   hiss

        Hiss of the Universe?
    fire-surf breaking on no shore
        except such ears as this?
                In
        ears shielded by Space
                (the vast
                Sparse)
        a thinned-by-distance din
        of roars of holocausts?

            Soon
        none to hear
            stars
            roar:
        the Universe
        less than a hiss

Bill Griffiths

For P-Celtic: found text from Machen

1

So she sat down
(A deep violet blue)

She began to kneed it
(of the brake)
She hid it under a big dock-
leaf
(covered)
She stood up
(and a clump)
She walked round the clay
(and when I think)

She got very red, her face
(and if I shut)
She took the clay in her hands
(the glaring sky)
She made the queerest doll
I had ever seen
(floating across it)

She said
if one loved very much,
the clay man was very good
if one did certain things
with it

2

(The sky was)
She took the clay out of the
bucket
(And in the middle)
She turned it about
(was a great elder tree)

She brought it out again
(with blossoms)
She sat down
(of meadowsweet)
She was softly singing all the
time
(of that day)
She sat down again
(my eyes I can see)
She began to shape a doll
(with little clouds
very white)
She hid it under a bush

She said
if one hated very much,
it was just as good,
only one had to do different
things with it

from *Building: The New London Hospital*

Fragment I

Adventure
big buildings / mountains
cartoons

Alf who was always sleeping in strange places

50 KG more than ½ a hundredweight
my back adds it up / spinal sum

a bishop can hold an abbey in one hand

trial chord
a boot shot out the door with a yell
there was a 2nd boot
& a birdcage

ya he screamed
drumming on the chute and too
rushed round to grin on the levellers
maybe they like it, that humour

A VISION of
Polly Polly notion
for own wife, came into

Fragment 4

little Jo wakes me up
with kick a little poke a kid laugh
I go an' twist Alf's feet (a bit more malice)
later bang on Pete's window
an come an try an think up an excuse for me.
No.

Each order's a
puzzle.

maybe I work my own work out.

Scrape on out

beeches
whizzing by
reddish red
my new boots
are as good as gold

Shepherd's Calendar

I follow her into the front room
I leave the sheep in the back room

what wld be really good
go an' sell all Tong church

wolf in one hand dog in one hand
no it's useless to separate 'em

everyone wantz a party
today I pretend I'm counting

to be helpful
I lead all the fish up-river right into the boats

maybe I shld get back even
to shovelling the sand

hang on
try yr head in the helmet

Fragment 9

1   go to Zoo
    draw
    watch Telly
    play

hope me Mum wakes up
read me a story

2   coat
    two
    three
    two
    coat
    sweets

3   go to sleep
    settle stomach
    go to market
    buy boots
    visit T'ronto
    go to seaside

4   go out tonight
    go out tomorrow
    go out for a ride on a bike
    get a new motor-guzzi
    move

Fragment 11

My latest thought brick for an abundant supply for home and clothes is being magnificently met. We have all had lots of new clothes and many items for our home.

I find it amazing how many of my thought bricks are fulfilled.

My latest thought brick has just materialized. My young son has been made a member of the local golf club.

I have had so many thoughtbricks . . . I was asked the other day if I would take over selling a special piece of equipment.

Even my thoughtbrick for a new sewing machine . . . one is now on its way from a friend who no longer needs hers.

A skin complaint has cleared up . . . in response to thoughtbrick techniques.

Fragment 12

For example, taking the cement onto palettes, for the hoist

For example, c'lecting the droppings to the chute

For example, catching bricks to stack

For example, carrying the long trunkings down the steps

For example, eating bacon

Shifting the poles under the skips

Smell of dust, cloud and chaser

Watching chasers moving about masks

Piping, shaped to wiring

C'lecting aly too, some little copper

Just LIFTING some things

Fragment 13

Maple
oak or ash
chaff or sawdust
lime and two of rubble

mask of rust
red vest
(catch the brix)
not o'molten blood

Fragment 18

Met Noel at Cheshire Street
out of boots my size

freed somehow of my jacket

out of my boots
now I can see you, it's sunshiny

Shepherd's Calendar cont'd.

A rich jigsaw'd gorse
ruby / lamb-yellow on a sandy land, & dry lunch

surrounded by a 100 wheeling dinosaurs, at
an aviary

gaunt legs of rubbish, pliant of bone
set up working under the rainarch

looking to see what is out there

The Ship

I am whale-in.
Ribs reach them over-across
We built them shaped so,
for a lovely roof
ply'ed
lined
plum-resin-soak to save wood
and it is all a fools' ship
so gross the water
and the rain lies.

Raw
we rub chest with chest
to be tribes that spark
whose the tubes/veins
inter-ring and branch us
thru

These are the chords, the crowd,
the hot hymn singing—
that the ships should sail
gauze-mauve
white-lemon

life-links

Something is missing:
foam poem
which is layers & layers
sun-bright and crumb-likest.

I do not mean
great house-side-size pearls
but the tiny-ortant
                    seeds of democracy

To be no arch of the church,
piddle-state,
no shaper, cute grave of the hill
(slicescape)
at all but

To dwindle
                : nought
to lack name / 'nown
leave nothing.
Isn't that?
(jus'
dandy)

South Song

Rejoice, join
be a Jute—
are people of water, corn-land,
oil-hills, work-towns;
made mazes, end-thickets,
walls in bald yellow-punched broom,
broad-roads.
ships, at a 1000 a week,
bring in stories
bonk sand-bells,
team with lorry-lights
and to be turf to football on,
roofs to bed under.

One of the 4 beasts saying
Come & see!
a white horse
and a crown
the noise of thunder
as it were
take peace
wheat at a penny
three measures
a great sword
under the altar
for the testimony
rest yet.

Alan Halsey

from *A Robin Hood Book*

XXI

Weakened by loss of blood Robin's last act was to slash his sword on Red Roger's neck: he was a famous murderer, Robert Hood, as well as Little John, together with their accomplices from among the dispossessed, about 1266 or 1283 or in Lionheart's time, say 1194. In this year would Jerusalem be taken and signs known as forest in full leaf of the third age coming of the holy spirit meaning love between rich and poor and new freedom among men. In the decade of Arnaut his lady and *trobar clus*. The date of his death 24 kal dekembris 1247 was no time at all just as his greenwood was a blank on the map or else he was truly King of Misrule whose wildnesse named him robin heud. He wounded his stepfather to death at plough: fled into the woods where *there is no deceit nor any bad law* and was relieved by his mother till he was discovered.

It was a time when the forests were being eroded from within by enclosure of land for out-of-town development and ring-roads. As the century came to an end retail parks and industrial estates proliferated. Between February **** and July **** there were fifteen commissions of *oyer and terminer* occasioned by raids on business parks, Tescos and Texas Home Care and attacks on quangoists and hypermarketeers. And Robyn hod in scherewod stod, hodud and hathud and hosut and schod: his four and thuynti arowus like jingling spells against prestige employment developers. He gadered and assembled unto him many misdoers beynge of his clothinge and, in manere of insurrection, wente into the wodes and strange contrays as outelawes, waitynge a tyme to murdre, sclee, and other grete harmes in that contray to do.

Happy Robin Whood coming to Lyndric falls asleep and hath a strange Dream there. Which at his awaking, he relates to his Companions, and then tells them that he is resolved forthwith to turn Hermit. Robin retires to Depe Dale, chuses the penitent Thief for his Patron, and spends the Remainder of his Time in great Penance and Devotion. He falls sick of a fever, Repairs to Kirklees to be let Blood. His mind consoled his endurable time slips away. Again he is lying in Little John's arms, it is a dream within a Barnsdale dreaming: again there is a thief in the forest, now a rival shaman in Gisborne's disguise *clad from head to foot in the hide of a horse*, a bloody mire of a path through the maze of trees Robin alone knew by weird aiming of his aimless arrow and the dream within the dream before that when he was captured in Nottingham not saving Marian who first named him a'Hood but kneeling as he must before the one in whose image his deere ladye was.

Thomas A. Clark is invited to lecture to the Sheriff's officers: *It is not the forest we eventually discover but our own strategies of evasion.* The officers' problem is that out in the forest they lose any sense of *their own*: even their strategies of evasion are stripped away and put to good use by the man or many they call Robin Hood. For either Robin Hood is himself the forest or Robin Hood is nobody at all. Some of the officers will have discovered for themselves the awful darkness of the forest night, that darkness of which brigand Robin is patron saint and lord protector. For *When men let light into the forest*, the teacher continues, *darkness hid in their hearts.*

XXII

A Saracen SAS or Assasseen called Nasir claims on HTV that once he had ridden with Robin Hood. The same programme also claims that Will Scathelocke changed his name to Scarlet after he had murdered his wife, but this was long before he joined the merry men and in any case he says it was de Rainault's boys set him up. He seems to connect it with some trouble at a building site and the bypass wrecking an otherwise unidentified town he calls Loxley. He is described as *angry, irritable, unreasonable, unfriendly and unhelpful.* Even his own father, he bangs down his fist, wasn't a worse bastard than Richard Coeur-de-Lion. We are spared an account of his drug addiction but in unused footage he tells how he once saw the heart of Sherwood open out and encompass the known world in a never-ending nonesuch glade. Instead the film cuts from Will aiming blind and hitting bullseye to a raid on hyperbole transfigured as the business park at Clun.

The sugared violence is detailed grain by grain as befits our peak viewing time. There is coverage of Marian's visionary powers, speculation on the occult meaning of the May Day rites and a modish take on the question *witch or wise woman.* But the dominant idea is that in the second period of greenwood days there was a second Robin Hood, not a yeoman reborn but Huntingdon's right heyre. Anthony Munday polishes a blade and downs another pint in the darkest recess of Amos Scathelocke's alehouse in Lichfield. He knows the Scathelocke brothers gave Huntingdon the lead. Seven years they ran wild and as he likes to say scaped malice before Huntingdon sprang them from Nottingham gaol or anybody ever heard the name Robin Hood.

Lord Tennyson who saw that *strange starched stiff creature Little John* kiss Kate, the same girl Munday had always called Jinny, sits beside him. They remember the banquets in Huntingdon's hall before that Worman or Warman of a steward was bribed on either hand to betray him. Remember Scarlet's wife he left dead or alive for the following of Robin's deere ladye. They laugh together about some of these recent stories: of Robin and Marian's travels in the East, Little John's appointment as Sheriff of Nottingham and the former Sheriff's daughter's later career as Prioress of Kirklees. But of his lordship's account of the fairies' retreat north out of Sherwood presaging the end of forest games poor Munday looks less than convinced.

XXIII

His acre. His arbour.

His ball, barn and barrow. His bay. His bog, his bow, his bower and but. His butts.

His cap. His castle. His cave and chair. His chase. His close. His court. His croft and his cross.

His delight.

His farm and his field.

His games. His garlands. His gate. His golden prize. His grave.

His hills and his howl.

His inn. His island.

His larder and leap.

His meadow, his mile and his moss.

His park. His penny stone. Pennyworths. Picking rods. Pot.

His rock.

His stable and stoop. His stride.

His table, his tales and his tower.

His valour.

His walk and his well. His wind. His wood.

XXIV

32*s*. 6*d*. for the chattels of Robert Hod, fugitive, Michaelmas 1230 at York. Green for the fairies, red for the witch. They two bolde children came to blacke water and we weepen for his deare body.

Amo Locksley.

Little John's been all over the place since Robin Hood died: his soul, he often says, sped from his body as arrow from bow but whether he means Robin's soul or his own nobody is ever quite sure. He showed the crowd a few tricks in Ostman-towne-greene by Dublin and he holed up in Murrayland and then headed home to lay himself down by his master's grave at Kirklees. They buried his bones of an uncommon size where he died in the precincts of Barnesdale of the fever at Hathersage.

Late us caste the stone
Late us caste the exaltre

The song itself wholly new and never before printed. To a doleful tune, lovelord Allin for Eleanor a-lorn. With a hey daring down a dale under this most ancient lime more fitting than oak for his trysting place ten as one foresters dance efter the auld wikit maner of Robene Hude while abbot and justice leap to it. *I made a chapel in Bernysdale where my sweet Marian lies buried.* I got me to the woods, Love followed me. He intertained an hundred tall men, and good archers with such spoiles and thefts as he got, upon whom four hundred (were they never so strong) durst not give the onset.

We'll get the next day from Brecknock the book of Robin Hood. Luellen King of Wales and Master of Misrule with his common cursitors whooden as Roberdsmen in Hobbehod form. They came to the Euro Park with torches lit and while the flames went up they were green in green and red on green received once more into the forest.

104

Lee Harwood

A Poem for Writers

To finally pull the plug on the word machine,
to rise from the chair late one evening
and step back into the quiet and darkness?

The dull white lights of the control-room of
a large hydro-electric dam in Russia
a computer centre in Brighton
the bridge of a giant oil tanker in the Indian Ocean.
Subdued light that reaches every corner
with no variation, tone, or shadow.

To leave the warm desk-light's tent
and step out into the . . .
     'I am just going outside and may be some time, Scottie'

Trains rush through the night,
across country through suburbs past factories oil refineries dumps,
the lights from their windows quickly disturbing the dark fields and woods
or the railway clutter as they pass through town,
staring in at the bare rooms and kitchens
each lit with its own story that lasts for years and years.
A whole zig-zag path, and the words stumble and fidget
around what has happened.

To walk out one January morning across the Downs
a low mist on the hills and the furrows coated with frost,
the dew ponds iced up.
The cold dry air.
And the sudden excitement when a flock of partridges starts up
in front of you and whirrs off and down to the left,
skimming the freshly ploughed fields.

'O ma blessure' groan the trees
with the wounds of a multitude of small boys' penknives.

No, not that—
but the land, the musics, the books
always attendant
amongst the foolish rush and scramble for vainglory,
talk or noise for its own sake, a semblance of energy
but not necessity.

Throw your cap in the air, get on your bike, and pedal off
down hill—it's a joy with no need of chatter,
Hello Chris.

Czech Dream

1

'The last bell is ringing
The fairy tale is over'
        shout some distant Czechs
        early on a frosty evening

"A sharp new moon
  in a smudged pink sky"
the story begins,
but seemed a repeated story
heard too many times before.
That tale over,
but another continues?

        "Arm in arm with you"?

2

The story began

    "Waking at five and passing into a jumble
    of dreams that with time ended by
    taking me into your arms.

    Over the weeks apart our minds race
    ahead of our bodies.
    When we meet, when they catch up,

then like a golden light, yes?
descends upon us wholly.

The dream is right.
The words wrong-foot sometimes
but try to push through the briars,
leap over them sometimes,
Brer Rabbit and all."

But I built too much in those dreams?
Too many scars and losses behind us.
Yet this chance, come upon by accident,
precious but shakey.

3

Not the village wedding, the mad bride's suicide,
billowing white veils against the greenery
of leaves or water

but

    "The thought of being with you.
    Dizzy floating I bite my lip
    in the middle of 'worldly commerce'."

4

" 'God has many mansions' said Miss Flanagan S.R.N.
  and the mansion where we dwelt . . .
  'and which mansion did you sleep in?' she added
                              with a sly laugh
  The rosaries and mugs of sherry are duly told
  Our love stained sheets tell
  our mansion"

5

Yet it doesn't shelter us
stave off the unavoidable collapse.
Dreams and stories snare us
before we can get past rubbing our eyes.
A mess of fears sets in that neither

Venus nor Ganymede can dispel.
Like Cupid a blind romantic rush
tips us sprawling into a mirrored room
where self-absorbed dreamers wander
almost ghostlike.
The creators of such illusions
stand close beside us. The creatures.

6

Spoken into a mirror

   "I travel to you

      your warmth
      To stand or lie in each other's arms

      battle scars, tired of the old deceits
      we come nervously to each other
      yet surely (we think)

      Is this the clarity
      we dream of?

      Not magic but more powerful
      in its simplicity—
      us

      Guided out beyond the ramparts
      the savage boors

      Touch me   you"

and tinkling bells in the distance
and the words flatter themselves, words on words,
and the first flakes of snow falling softly,
the landscape whitening out

Michael Haslam

from *Continual Song*

01
84

WINGS
   in a blank white shining room
blind me so I blanch and flinch
and blink still at the white
of walls and floor.

   Wings of The Idea
    of the Advance of Being
Human, sprouting from a Sphere.

A zephyr rushing
 to the visible from the invisible
and filling lungs.

A falcon falling out upon the wind—
the vocal remnant of illumination so sustained
until it disappears inaudibly.
   Here, take these token wings,
an interruption to an argument,
a stop upon an outrage and an anger;
may they carry you through areas
of Spiritual Danger—

   the infernal haunt that hurts internally,
and funnily enough I must be blanked with wings
of wishing prayer, '*May the Planet
be washed also with these wheeling winds.*'

30
55

The chisel slid, I hit my little knuckle
on the chamfer edge, and bright red globes
of blood accumulate, and with the clouding
they coagulate, and six doves swoosh
        to seal the suffering, the pain, the sore,
the harmony of vanished worlds on fire.

Each Word The Dead shout through
The Trumpet of The Ear has been distorted.
Through an utter wizardry the sun is turning blue.
It was a dreamer going into code
        in coded gloom. Lunatic
Window-Wall Proportions. Dead Loud Shouting
        Echoes in the Shape of Things,
along the avenue, the prospect of a
clouding of an ear.

The pain bout clamours more inaudibly.
Some people die of a broken heart.
The day she drove the van away it seemed
the fabric of the land had ripped
and I was standing in her slipstream bare
but for my tatters in the wind.
        Look after thyself, then.
Loud Shouting Echoes in the Shape of Things.
Small clouds of sweat evaporating swiftly
vanish in the heat.
I am the keeper of my body and my love.
I seek a cigarette, a break,
        a left-hand glove.

No Bloody Matter
43
42

The slightest vacuum when the concrete-mixer stops
before the birds return the song of wild exactness

as a cartridge to the chamber
opens a gracious jewel atmosphere of space:
Amazing Reservoir! The miles and miles
of water pouring through
to no point in retrieval.

Water consciousness is sound, and listening
I'm weird in thought and scents of peace
between the breaks.

Each day I'm thought
by themes of hurt
and beat my fists in air and take
Tobacco,

until signs are made to dowse me through
an avenue into a perfect chamber.

Here as a slave I wash my sloths out
in a water music enclave, while
all sorts of sorry doors and courtyards
safe from breezes
ring with antique charm.
And quiet in the centre of a circle
in the square appears
a whole side of the body-image
weeping or disintegrating,
bleeding like a fire at the extremes.

84
01

Writing in a nearly lightless loft,
my candle lost, my last two matches spent.
Dark flux over the woodstove, skylight luminosity—
Corona Borealis. And a draught of air
takes shape around the trapdoor,
wafting with the scent of hay, —*Come to me!*
Conjured out of nothing: Love
is meant to be loved to be sane, if only
Phoenix multiply my days.

Fingers untie the blind.
I'm home and standing in my doorway
as I wash my face with a wet white flannel
drink a cordial of spring-water and lime
and wish the day,
     reflecting on the valley tone of bell,
the couple of our sexual scufflings
in the natural dark, I wish the light,
and it's the skirling lark
vaulting her spectrous speech into the sky—
like that I wish to hear The Phoenix sing
     through my beginning heart of wind and blues,
along a memory of avenue, a querying
Revolt against The Zodiac,
Attacking Keys
     leads the excruciating silver
into shiver till
     the practice is perfected
metaphor

and to continually sing,

Randolph Healy

Primula veris

Clustering atop a leggy stem
ten elf green bodices tapered down
to blown about yellow pinafores.

Near the ground a mob of blotched leaves,
belching and gulping, stiff with liquor,
watched constellations kink and bend
and languages drift from grammar to grammar.

Sister Mary's favourite flower
cast a light on all the goudgers
that she coaxed, effing and blinding,
to various degrees of joined-up writing.

One great arching cadence
glosses the world as a double spiral
speaks to itself with epochs for clauses

root shoot and flower
stitching together the heavens and the earth.

Mutability Checkers

The full deck gusts outside the playground
briefly forming an aerial house of cards.
I see a woodlouse chasing a tiger,
and square pegs in square holes.
An atom is the part of your throat that sticks out.
Every Saturday, I am a bicycle.
Famous Dialogues lie on a table.
Enter Socrates, winged by the medium's
dot to dot. Solvent without solution,
ignoramus champ of all history,

I think of you sending away a would-be
empiricist with a flea in his ear,
then sweeping to the end of the argument—
reality as a series of diagrams.
Secateured titan, I dreamed a random river
whose surface's inflexions shimmered
with every possible geometry
where all-envisaging blindness hatched
and crossed as chance, swollen with potential,
surged against the given, sculpting a world
where botched and sublime bloomed without design.

The Size of This Universe

There are more stars in the universe
than all the words ever spoken,
as many stars as atoms in a matchstick.

Tonight, standing in earth's shadow,
close your eyes and see
that this universe is itself a statement
within which every statement made
is partial and uncomprehending,
that every detail suggests a total
at which one may not arrive,
that no amount of words
countable in a human lifetime
can absolutely express truth,
that no finite number of truths is sufficient
to check all possible propositions.
Incomplete.
Uncertain.
When I was first told that air is made of atoms
I worried for days about what was between them,
frightened of nothing.
Mintaka, Alnilam, Alnitak,
Orion's tilted belt.
Without uncertainty matter would collapse.
Silence.
The quantum vacuum
is brimming with particles

agitated
continually bubbling forth
in pairs annihilating
nothing in ferment
hir eien brennynge and cleer-seynge
over the comune myghte of men.

The edges are moving out at almost the speed of light.
All the stars
all the matter in the universe
to the space available
are as one grain of sand to the Atlantic.
Some talk of a bubble
in a foam of universes.
Look out for
Silence.

John James

Bye Bye Blackbird

for Douglas Oliver

over the clay-laden estuary a
soft grey light comes sneaking
my heart away it is the spirit of Colne Spring

& all along the shoreline an oyster-catcher
dips & bobs a splashing blur of black & white
against the easterner

curlews ghosting by a little above the fleet
fly our souls out of perversity

Brightlingsea has grown where it is the sepia
gaff-rigged sails of the smacks manoeuvre away

into the Dutch hinterspace beyond Mersea Island a rich
alluvium gets itself laid over years we mooch along

towards a frith
dreaming of sprats & opals

Sister Midnight

stuttering rain at the window
early in autumn your breast
loosed from its hold
the caprice of your lifting thighs
the serious depth to your smile
I seem made of insubstantial elements like a leaf
the otherwise silent house occasionally sways
two blocks away the river seeps from lock to lock
the telephone obdurate & yellow against the blue rug
the gale now pulling the whole room apart at the seams

hungover leaves fill up the dusty often
can't do anything at all at other times
you just don't care at all you try it
your own way her face a little blue that shaky
girl with the shaky hand can't hold the pen
too weak for the desk the lower chair
the lower sky hurry by on the pavement outside
everything slipping away with the day
which is closing in on itself at 3:58 the sky
all lit up between a crack in the buildings
& under those clouds lie the chimneys
decorated with a fretwork of little birds
& large grey washes of sky over the gables

the bell rings but I refuse to answer
I might have been a painter but there was an accident
in my life right down the line of a fierce fatigue
replete with overcoats my cherry which is why it is worst
when you have forgotten the mayonnaise remember
I told you there'd be something funny about it she said
like her potatoes of lead, flash flash, alas a
cold pallor has overcome my scrotal sac
in the sharp gusts of autumn in all those places
I said I'd never go again & then did
as if I'd never even forgotten
                              meanwhile
your head my little sweetheart of the steppes
don't hesitate grab the momentum while the going's good
sink to your knees beside the yellow sofa
take him between the folds of my bright magenta wraparound
the bright glossy oval of a knee & remarkable vest
rippling up over my becoming
the casual spectator of hoydens in the sharp grass of the park
steam rises from the coffee cups
the wine splashes into the little glass
a vigorous red in keeping with the tone
of all that battles to be without my arm
oh my arm in this smallest minute where I enter your name
for the aim of the race do you know
there are certain sounds which tear at my liver
like a cat at its matted fur & a certain
absence of detail has for the first time
featured in my life tightening my collar

& lurking near the black marble of Italian headstones
shining back at the bright little windows of the local
do-it-yourself shops in the rising morning
like a sickness that imprisons the heart in a fettered glove
& now I recognize your great talent as a member of the
human race as the peasant offers me the plastic salt-box
& I look around for the snuff of the father
painted in green & embroidered in my vest
as a text for my meditations

outside the window the trees move in the night
your grand desire rises in my throat & my heart
pulses on into its thirty-sixth year like an indifferent
steam-engine while milky tea embalms the organ
a woman feels very cold around the buttocks
once in a while & yet your laugh brings light to me
cause you're the first good man I've found
pressing the glossy black embellishments to the hand
under the gentle curtain imagery of the gasfire & the
dusty smell of old red velvet cinema seats
                    but still this hanging over
                    of the female in the man
                    means maybe
                    rather than
& that's not the end but a beginning like when
you can't turn the key any further in the sardine can
& all along the edge of the skyline
the last green cringe of daylight
drops like a plate to the ground

Shakin All Over

dip your head in the basin & go
walking the early morning streets late March rotting
from the inside out leather under
dog-tooth green check tweed
lathering the aching in the rib-cage just got to be
got up & gone I'm not turning away I'm
not looking down I'm puzzling over
the influence of the Stickies I
freely enter your special unit I

don't look down
light drapes flap at the covered windows
touch at the hairs at the back of the hand
the shackling of trucks in the sidings rattle of
curtain rings & soon I hear that crazy fluttering sound
cut through an otherwise absolutely silent room
it's the undertones
of your vibration rattle of pink noise
the poise with which you set your arm alight
our mutual pride &
randomly chosen limited isolation

oh baby what a place to be to disregard
the giant hoard of wounds this tress
in the creaking of copper ear-rings
strands pins & hair-slides & drinking Black Bush
a wave of dark air rolls through the barley
& then you can recall it all &
jet discs rattle as you walk
close to the shifting metacentre
that stripe in your wrist where
the heat is still fresh &
reckless of the edge your face as pale as
quartz or gypsum you're turning backwards
to a new scene as the lozenge dissolves into
crossover & he leisters the jumping thigh
with whatever comes to hand a beer-can amber or zip
the flax caught in the teeth of the comb
& she cries out for once & for all
churning the mud in the pool

                        & later
in the studded augury of bar-tables in the Midland
the immediate future appears strictly female there
will be somebody to talk to & I like to look at you
without somebody watching over us happy &
glorious & even under close escort
the narrow band of pouncing
will be hidden in the skin
                        & we'll be
lapping up a sleek pony
eye rolling over a speckled back zigzag
the stun-shot sways you as you stay on top

they say you'll never be free
but give me your hand here
under the duress of sliding straps
the tang of the white bush
the linen spattered with honey & lager
the dawn spouting with little birds & pressing
a shoulder-blade to the mattress
& there's not so much as a bit of boiling pig
left to be eaten the coverlet hoods you
squinting into the sunlight the talk
twirls at your throat & your hard green
is painted with flashing white
emulsion disinfectant as you apply an orange
towel to the stomach the neck the
perforated magma warm & moist & groaning

Idyl

tiny fish
start from her knee

just below
the amber glow

of lapping sea
in Brittany

another year of heavy dreams
the smell of slurry everywhere

a potato farl a cup of tea
too hot to sip

a drifting film of yellow sky
cold in the north

a sudden ease
driv in the vein

inches of soda bread
adorn the plate

the farmer's son goes off to perform
in the milking parlour

later we dispatch another bull
in father's honour

each with a glass or two
before the night

whiskey & water & a small cigar
echo echo

"hello boys
it's me again

I come to greet you
far & when

the horizon opens like a door
the speed of light is not a possible speed

for a person cannot overtake light
what can never be reached so

heart break tomorrow
it ain't always sorrow

the line knows where it's going
& we know we're going with it

I leave the rest to you
distance no object

Amryl Johnson

from *Rainbow Dragon Trilogy*

Oil on Troubled Waters
(The People's Calypso)

We rose like a phoenix
towards the song
Shackles now a vague echo
our pain a dull throb
Sailing into a future
where hopes are fulfilled
We stepped off the boat
to find ourselves wading through
oil on troubled waters
glowing, glaring deception of the truth
Oil on troubled waters
Rebuff—resent—reject—refuse—repel

Colours can be fickle
with no sense of esteem
We know of seven who will
go with almost anything
They'll cling to steel
They'll cling to glass
Dead, rotting fish
They'll even cling fast to
oil on dirty water
Mirage of the promises and dreams
Oil on troubled waters
Recant—recoil—revoke—repress—restrict

Ribbons of colour
in filthy streams
shimmer on the surface
while they masquerade

as a rainbow island
This mass of bright rays
deceive the senses until
you're hypnotised by the sight of
oil on muddy waters
Paralysed by the facets of pretence
Oil on troubled waters
React—revolt—reveal—retort—resolve

A better life
with opportunities
where the shade of your skin
doesn't stunt your growth
But we got the worst jobs,
living conditions
When we speak they say
they can't understand
Oil on troubled waters
You can't go back and say you have failed
Oil on troubled waters
Rent—repair—repaint—recognise—remain

Shock almost
robs your ambition
The swindle seems complete
when experience teaches words
you get to learn well
They offer "nigger" "discriminate"
"marginalise" "menial"
"black bastards" and "repatriate"
Oil on troubled waters
Your vocabulary is now almost complete
Oil on troubled waters
Reconsider—regret—rebuke—rethink—resign

The window to our souls
in this hostile land
looks onto night which has
no moon nor stars
Our thoughts, the restless
curtains in this dark,
twitch with every wind
to writhe and squirm

Oil on midnight waters
We shudder in every passing breeze
Oil on troubled waters
Reproach—remorse—retreat—remnant—remote

Drabber than ever
cold invades each flake
to stab, twisting like
icicles near the root
of each scale
He hasn't stopped shivering
since we arrived
How can late summer still feel so cold?
Oil on troubled waters
No heatwave could ever warm this chill
Oil on troubled waters
Recover—reprieve—remedy—recoup—rescue

Ultra-violet would
improve this plight
So standing with a crystal
to the spectrum, he
tried to tempt light
into shards of colour
slivers for his scales
He tried hard but they would not stay
Oil on troubled waters
Colours kept fading back to white
Oil on troubled waters
Reflect—reflex—relay—refract—retain

We channelled out hopes
through long-frosted years
trying to coax apathy
towards eventual response
Hardworking Christians
in the motherland
want to be accepted
Is that too much to demand?
Oil on troubled waters
Rigid. They would barely yield or budge
Oil on troubled waters
Resilient—religious—reconcile—reason—relate

Curving through circles
from this spiral of pain
we provoke the ashes
of recent victories
Spirited people
of endurance and generosity
wiping dust from the drum
we summoned the 'mas to traverse
oil and troubled waters
We've done it once, we can rise again
Oil and troubled waters
Recall—repeat—revive—remember—reclaim

On the streets of Port-of-Spain
when freedom came
we beat the French
at their own game
Fusing strong links of culture
fashioned an intricate medley
so unique and inventive
it confirms the essence of creativity, diffusing
oil and troubled waters
We forged an image which will survive
Oil on troubled waters
Rekindle—restore—recover—rectify—retrieve

Beak, a scythe of bright silver
sharpened diamonds are his claws
His sequined wings span the centuries
serpenting dagger for a tail
Eyes are the burning furnace of memory
At the most quiet, tranquil time of year
we rage him loose on the
streets of Notting Hill, engulfing
oil and troubled waters
It is the symbol of our will to overcome
Oil and troubled waters
Revive—resume—rehearse—relish—rejoice

Linton Kwesi Johnson

Mi Revalueshanary Fren

mi revalueshanary fren is nat di same agen
yu know fram wen?
fram di masses shatta silence —
staat fi grumble
fram pawty paramoncy tek a tumble
fram Hungary to Poelan to Romania
fram di cozy cyaasle dem staat fi crumble
wen wi buck-up wananada in a reaznin
mi fren always en up pan di same ting
dis is di sang im love fi sing:

Kaydar
e ad to go
Zhivkov
e ad to go
Husak
e ad to go
Honnicka
e ad to go
Chowcheskhu
e ad to go
just like apartied
will av to go

awhile agoh mi fren an mi woz taakin
soh mi seh to im:

wat a way di eart a run nowadays, man
it gettin aadah by di day
fi know whey yu stan
cauz wen yu tink yu deh pan salid dry lan
wen yu teck a stack yu fine yu ina quick-san
yu noh notice ow di lanscape a shiff
is like valcanoe andah it an notn cyaan stap it
cauz tings jusa bubble an a bwoil doun below

strata sepahrate an refole
an wen yu tink yu reach di mountain tap
is a bran-new platow yu goh buck-up

mi revalueshanary fren shake im ed an im sigh
dis woz im reply:

Kaydar
e ad to go
Zhivkov
e ad to go
Husak
e ad to go
Honnicka
e ad to go
Chowcheskhu
e ad to go
jus like apartied
will av to go

well mi nevah did satisfy wid wat mi fren mek reply
an fi get a deepa meanin in di reaznin
mi seh to im:

well awrite
soh Garby gi di people dem glashnas
an it poze di Stallinist dem plenty prablem
soh Garby leggo peristrika pan dem
canfoundin bureacratic strategems
but wi haffi face up to di cole facks
im also open up pandora's bax
yes, people powa jus a showa evry howa
an evrybady claim dem demacratic
but some a wolf an some a sheep
an dat is prablematic
noh tings like dat yu woulda call dialectic?

mi revalueshanary fren pauz awhile an im smile
den im look mi in mi eye an reply:

Kaydar
e ad to go
Zhivkov

e ad to go
Husak
e ad to go
Honnicka
e ad to go
Chowcheskhu
e ad to go
just like apartied
will av to go

well mi couldn elabarate
plus it woz gettin kinda late
soh in spite a mi lack af andahstandin
bout di meanin a di changes
in di east fi di wes, nonediless
an alldow mi av mi rezahvaeshans
bout di cansiquenses an implicaeshans
espehshally fi black libahraeshan
to bring di reaznin to a canclueshan
ah ad woz to agree wid mi fren
hopein dat wen wi meet up wance agen
wi coulda av a more fulla canvahsaeshan

soh mi seh to im, yu know wat?
im seh wat? mi seh:

Kaydar
e ad to go
Zhivkov
e ad to go
Husak
e ad to go
Honnicka
e ad to go
Chowcheskhu
e ad to go
jus like apartied
soon gaan

Tom Leonard

100 Differences Between Poetry and Prose

poetry stops before the end of the margin
you can talk about prose without mentioning school
you don't read poetry to get from Glasgow to Saltcoats without noticing

John Menzies doesn't stock poetry
whoever heard of war & peace having the line as a unit of semantic yield
you can call a poem what you want and say its poetic licence

poetry is the subliminal history of linguistic shape
ahem
poetry has four wheels, two wings and a pair of false teeth

poetry is the heart and the brain divided by the lungs
poetry is the world's oldest cock and fanny story

you don't get prose in anapaestic dimeters
nobody publishes their first slim volume of prose
aristotle never wrote The Proses

if you dribble past five defenders, it isn't called sheer prose
poets are the unacknowledged thingwaybobs

poetry is quintessentially contrapuntal
the square root of poetry is an ever-evolving quark
whenever Vergil looked in the mirror, he beheld an epic Latin poet

poetry is all the juicy bits in the juiciest order
poetry is jellied religion
pascal: if your labourers complain too much, try taking them to a poetry reading

prose goes scchhpludd
prose goes scchhpludd scchhpludd clomp clomp clomp
are you sitting comfortably

then I'll end

song

yi surta
keep trynti avoid it thats
thi difficult bitty it

jist
no keep findn yirsell
sitn

wotchn thi telly ur
lookn oot thi windy

that wey yi say
christ a could

go a roll n egg
ur
whuts thi time fuck me

wiv nay
cookn oil nwi need
potatoes

The Evidence

(Sheriff Court: Glasgow, April 1995)

I gave chase
to the appellant
with his bucket and billposters

and he fell, my lord,
on the point of my apprehending
him. At which point

I too fell down
—we had come to a grassy slope—
and coming to, I found

the appellant lying
with a bloodied face

on the adjacent path.

My colleague constable lindsay
who had herself fallen down
in the chase, saw nothing of this:

but she arrived in time to find
myself and the appellant
lying some feet apart.

That witness was lying
who said I stood over Mr Anwar
and kicked him where he lay;

nor did I tell the appellant:
"This is what happens
to black boys with big mouths".

The truth is that I felt sorry for him,
so I called an ambulance,
which I boarded with my colleague

and therein charged the appellant
under the Environment Protection Act, Scotland,
with the illegal posting of bills.

opting for early retirement

time only/
time management

reified agency
of cost-function conscience

numerical value
constantly

defining the scope
of being-in-the-structure

taboo being
unpredictable being

being as quantum
being as inefficient

motor tasks
establishing targets

recognising actual deficiencies
establishing potential deficiencies

guilty until innocent
the human as an agent of deficiency

the question always
and the answer always

surely total innocence is impossible

Before the 1820 rising in the West of Scotland a network of

don't call them government spies

call them MI5

call them MI6
call them special branch
call them the anti-terrorist squad
call them F1, F2, F3, F4, F5, F6 right through to 12
call them counter-insurgency

don't mention them
keep quiet about them
refuse to discuss how much money's spent
refuse to discuss what they do
swear everyone to secrecy

call them Intelligence

call the critics "unpatriotic"
call the critics "a security risk"
call the critics "conspiracy theorists"
call the critics "traitors"

call the critics *paranoid*

government spies kept watch over the Combination Acts against assembly

First Poster Poem against the Criminal Injustice Bill

Tony Lopez

A Path Marked with Breadcrumbs

The collapsed addict mother, passed out
Under a hedge in the nineteenth century
Knows the colonial economy
In point of fact. The child a sweet girl
Changes into gold out of pure virtue
In a novel by a woman called George.

Tell the age of a hedge by counting species
How long it takes the natives to move in.
For the consumption of opium or diet food
See *cultural ideal*, see *anorexic fix*.
There is a circuit in neurotic behaviour
Like racial fear in English Literature

Where grazing rights and planted enclosures
Are just real enough to be rented out.
You may continue to use your PIN code
In advance of the merger, even if
The false body image is politic,
Floating on corporate identity.

It is not enough to be on the fence
One must be inside using surveillance.
We live on a little muddy island
Grow rice, catch fish and care for our children.
Some very good submissive subjects
Only one previous family now deceased.

No Transport

The bid for a new majority.
Some maintenance needed on the house.
Water running away from the cisterns:
Radiant heat loss. A voice it was
Selling network marketing by phone.

Gather up poisoned slugs by hand.
They go hard and dry like catshit
Kill birds, frogs and hedgehogs.
Tell me (in public) the customers rule
Funding will follow to the cost centre:

Is anyone running the system? We have
A low use discount on the standing charge
Incoming only. Business opportunities.
Banks mail out schemes to lend us money
Do you sincerely want to be repossessed?
We have invented this government.

The children coming down with stress illness,
Mother shouting at them in the morning.
Father faces the wall, swallows beta-blockers.
What's happened to the family? It's called
A 'Building Society' and is an instrument
Of social improvement. You can eat dirt.

You can dream of another life far away.
They come into your living room at night
With garlands of flowers and bright teeth.
Then the warm embrace of a strange woman
With semtex strapped to her waist.

from *Assembly Point D*

Dauntless the slug-horn to my lips I set
Taking a stand for the names who had been
So badly treated by crowd behaviour in the market;
Whereas our man was calm, drew figures in the sand,
And spoke to them as individuals. The old guy
Putters on, his canvas in a trench, putting neat squiggles
On the big white primed sheets: a million each, believe it.
Cartoon prawns and crabs go into *Eurotunnel*
Singing along with zydeco music. Redwoods fall.
It was a teacher bound and gagged a four-year-old boy
With sticky tape labelled *Nastro Adesivo:* 3M
Holding back the late works to keep up the selling price.
Can you design a machine that turns coffee
Into urine? That daydreams of oral sex?

Our fortunes are in the stars, truly, since brokers
Are using astrology in the stockmarket. What price
Celestial backwardation (a little space to write and eat salad in)?
Shadowing the wives of ex-company presidents
In their dotage. The owl of Minerva begins her flight
Only as dusk is falling. My nerves are bad tonight.
This kind of gives closure to a long career in "Vice."
All famous names, all massive savings, every third one free.
The office has a fine view of cliffs and grassy hills.
You read INDUS OPAQUE as you stick out your tongue
Over where a new vine is beginning to cover the gazebo
Cut so many times before. [Clay animal noses here.]
Rose garden: black velvet: stalking donkey:
The banquet is at 3102 Main Street, 15th and Main.

Erasures and palimpsests are reduced to a flat
Surface effect: the afterlife of ethics.
A judge, a game-show host, bag-lady, dinner-lady,
Madman, murderer, banished king, politician,
Football manager, dentist, spoilt birthday-girl.
A few poor tatterdemalions made all this racket,
Howling in the night. Ugolino was there
Chewing a juicy walnut of brains from behind,
His arse positioned over the stunned polis.
Sing poor, sweet airlines. Scholars have paid lip-service

To the oral nature of poetry. We can see
Submissive women waiting on TV mountain tops:
Lovely silk dress in a helicopter shot. You'll need
Your velour passenger pillow and something to read.

This turning seems to go only to a business park.
You're on the bus tonight, headphones, synthetic waves,
Daryl Hall sings we've reached the borderline
By a terrace of little cottages made over *bijou*.
A large selection of other vehicles always available
Leaving Taunton on the M5. "Love will last forever."
In a thousand cities our offices are getting ready
To see that every transaction goes smoothly.
When the alarm sounds we go to assembly point D.
Agoraphobia, chronic anxiety, social phobia,
The narrator is bound up in some unspecified crisis.
When did the blue skies start to gather clouds?
How long have we poor shepherds lived and dreamed
Within these shady incremental pay-scales?

Rob MacKenzie

Like Pornography

get put gat   eisnin monocotyledon
stapled strong words panties   her burnished machair cunt

as if th'exigent marram   's fed up and hungry for
sea licks the billie lift yet   spat jizz distilling her bulimic

acid weak words proper   hald he noses toom
tart meat lace candy   fell sleekit in the buckled air

Blue Sky in Morning

for Katrina

Moon in a blue sky, morning loneliness, the need to have children.
Frost. First the waxed coat, then brittle shirt, undershirt and lungs
feel like leaves. ' later lost even the effect of cinema like rain.

The bike's a boy's evident skeleton amongst cars. Family fords and turbulence.
Each front room at the lights. Protection. Nothing's purposeful enough because
work and family do not commute, nor transport and connectivity. ' as well

the sky closes, moon disappears ' over the sake of relatives, and consolation.

square

this dancer's stance slapped solely f'r th'effect
of her vaudeville instancy 'at gobbles affectation.

this lip cliff fall int' a bright remove.

this sclim o' sized blond modernism glimpsed
from a train turned of thought to her limber dalliance.

this tricksy idem stretched i' my frame o' making sense.

Category Mistakes in Biochemistry

What Michaelmas collision'f penis-waggle existentialism, eugenics
an' the free market claims I can be all that I can be
'f I *just do it*? (Penis-waggle — there's itself if ever, but anyone
'll punch the air gin the header's sweet enough, and we're not all bad.)
The thrill o' the moment's like sex, sure,
but sex should not be type. Th'imperatives driving sex don't drive football,
commerce, nor even growing up. Th'imperatives driving sex don't even drive
all our sex: the sex industry's all reconstructed urge, not consequence.
Pumping sperm into prostitutes's no winning genetic strategy.

Th'appeal t'athwart potential's exactly adolescence as isolation: saleable,
feart only that our folks won't die before they get old,
'r that we'll have children.

The sweet, swift enthalpy release upon meeting the cross, far post,
has almost the functionality of sex. And hope, explaining the confusion.
It's a biochemical category mistake — which is itself a secondary structure:
genes read the small print — like status and satisfaction, accomplishment
and progress, example an' type, victory and th'unbounded life.

Glossary

billie: randy
fell: very
hald: home, den
idem: identity as sameness (Ricoeur)
jizz: semen

lift: sky
sclim: climb
sleeket: sleek, sly
toom: empty

Barry MacSweeney

Ode Long Kesh

     & tie strings together
        as the sky falls
between the knees, fragrant
  lard-mouth. A planet in decision. But
        falls sunless towards
  the best uncle, Flapless Man. Sheets & Arrows
on his bracken ankles, terse cloth
      in his worn digital pie. Last week's
Luddite, Tolpuddle broth of caps, Flapless
      leaks
           & the sky (his odd wife)
        fails to strangle inclinations
          between those sheeny
          thighs. Flapless
        never comes.
Flop goes Flapless & the whole arterial mess
         back by the gas with an
           Irish supper. No doubt
       the last of all marchers.
         Overliving the skin
        & out for the year.
     Nouveau Flapless in the garments of rich
     hunger, living on potatoes & nitro-glycerine.

Flame Ode

    'and the warm weather is holding'

          far back, whisky
      nailed the plate, he
kissed an Ace
         On into
overmuch, pukey niblets

in the shadow of the magic mushroom

children held rooms for grief in the mild autumn

And why won't he come, my mother in the pantry

flames shift
in the sky

working late in a crane
                              But, he did not, arrive, he
                              left

    & a crime-reporter reviewed my poems, the
    last bud

with a quote from mike mcclure

                    the lion roared back
              sleek beast

        flames
        factory gates

the blackmailer treads over the instruments

                    of the poor shift

people have to eat

Ode

    Urals post-master, this is your
dead child! Ecto-
lunch on the shore, spherical
& gorgeous.
              tattle for
a leaf, butter in your eyes
as you fall.
              a dream
of deltas in whose sunken shore

                  his weightless sister
          drives her car
                  of charity.   au bord de la
pollisonne rouge, he struck
                  the platform.

          rainy cheeks of the driver on the
          train at Koblenz, Monday
          of the year, a
          Swiss descendant dream.

              But
          clank   another
                  point to
          the maquis, altar
              in the offside, together
              by the feminine
                  time.

outside the violent plant.

watching the skaters' line
swell.

Far Cliff Babylon

1

          Far cliff Babylon, your natty dread future is a dole card
                  stamped with asteroids exploding
                  across the city of my
                      birth.

              Putty children,
              crassly aware.

              I am 16.
              I am a Tory. My

          vision of the future represents
              no people.

Celeriac priesthood offers up my rifle to the sky.

2

Tear the carbon paper of your soul. Virtue
lacking wit cries on the edge
of minefields.

Agents want me to yield. When
I see the Sex Pistols in my dreams I
roll into the garden of a small
nightmare,
looking for holidays in the
sun.

No fun.

My simple body is
a complicated asteroid,
torn
from her
skin.

My life is the size of a
pin.

I have no people.

They represent me.

When we go my separate ways
the colours are dark.

No more apartheid.

3

Hearts like aubergines
cancelled from the garden.

Bint glove,
suck the rivets from
my cymbal,
smoke
vermilion gas. Feel

the city like a river, its
future not written in
words.

Language is a steady stick.

But people are
colour conscious. Their
heroes are red and their traitors
yellow,
Dan Smith fruit skin.

I have cancelled everything and now I am free to choose.

4

I have died every day since I gave up poetry.
Dangerous condescending humans lapped it up.

They stuck their tongues into the gravy and
licked the plate.

Heroism learns to be a stranger
with odd shoes,
too late to use.

Combine your heart with fantasies
of power.
Copulate with the dynamoes inside this
red shirt.

Armband sex.

Helmets erect their tower.

Men train boys.
Fascist tarts obey.

5

Exaggeration is a gift that strays, towards
the minor forest of her mind.
Pineal furtherance smokes, like
a blues clarinet
in water.

She is my only daughter,
torn from her skin.

I would not let her in. I
discovered my ability as
a father
snapped at the wrist.

I ate my fist.

The doubts are bicycles in the
hospital door.

We sucked the floor.

6

The small belief is arrogant, how sick people
move. Hit my bruised runways,
on a council grant.

We collapse in domestic chaos.
Three minute punch ups are commonplace.

My children can
never pay back the thrashings
bashings & lashings.

I represent no people. Not even
myself.

Small,
crawling piety, you deserve
many bombs
&
guns.

I ate your Christian fish.
It made me sick.

Division is your prayer.

from *Pearl*

Pearl Says

Down from the rain-soaked law
and the rim of the world
where even on misty nights
I can see the little lights
of Penrith and Kendal and, yes,
Appleby, and hear the clatter of unshoed
horses which pound like my heart,
I also sense the moss greened underwater
stones of the Eden to the west. I trim
the wick for mam's asleep now, dad
long gone to Cumberland and work, and
read read my exercise books filled
with stories by Bar, my trout-catching
hero, dragons and space ships, sketches
in crayons you can't buy anymore.
When I stand on the top road and bow
in sleet, knuckle-bunching cold, or
slide over dead nettles on snow, do
not mistake my flung out silhouetted
limbs for distant arches and viaducts.
I am not bringing you legendary feats
of sophisticated engineering. I in
worry eat my fist, soak my sandwich
in saliva, chew my lip a thousand times
without any bought impediment. Please

believe me when my mind says and
my eyes send telegraphs: I am Pearl.
So low a nobody I am beneath the cowslip's
shadow, next to the heifers' hooves.
I have a roof over my head, but none
in my mouth. All my words are homeless.

The Shells Her Auburn Hair Did Show

for Stephen Bierley,
July 13, 1993

Good morning Pearl, good morning John,
good morning the Jesus Christ Almighty;
good morning Stephen, transferring
to the Alps from Lac de Madine:
I know your heart's in Helpston today.
Pearl walked barefoot down the rain-soaked flags last night, fearful
of smoke and fire, with words on the slate: Where do I go
to bang MY head? Where will I find a workshop
sustained by Strasbourg grants
and European funny money, with instruments
modern enough to replace the canyon in the roof of my mouth?
Government? What does that mean?
Stephen, best friend of Barry, travelling in France, father
of Rachel and Timothy, husband of Sarah, what
does a government do? Can it make you speak?
I leak truth like a wound, sore not seen to.
Call me a scab if you wish, I'm still plain Pearl.
Wild Knitting was named after me, I know you did, Bar.
Every day—I wake at four—tongue fever grasps me
and I am possessed: though
my screen is blank and charmless to the human core
I have an unbending desire to marry consonants and vowels
and mate them together
in what you call phrases and sentences
which can become—imagine it—books!
I'd like to sit down with Stephen, inside the borage groves, sing him
my songs of the stream.
But of course I cannot.
My cuticles above singular fields

of harvested grain, when torched stubble is nowhere
near the heat of the burning grief
in my illiterate heart, when I can only hope to extinguish it
with unfettered tears, at four in the morning, when no one else
is awake.
I walk to the wetted garden where the lawn is short.
All the skies are leased anyway. Nothing is owned
by humans. It is an illusion nightmare.
You fall through the universe
clinging to unravelled knots and breaking strings.
John eating grass. Percy drinking brine.
No B&Q in my day. No proper ABC.
My mouth a wind-tunnel. I flew like a moth in its blast.
Take my hand and put me right.
This is the end of the bulletin from the end of the road.

Pearl Alone

Yes, I am not emitting articulate sound
I take my stand and — deliberately — refuse to plead.
There is no adoration in my mute appeal.
My tongue a pad or cone for the trumpet's bell.
Tongue-tied, bereft of ABC, I lap
and soak my whistle at the law's rim.
In mood moments
I say smash down the chalkboard:
let it stay black.
Shake my chained tongue, I'll fake a growl — a-a-a-a-.
Dog my steps, I am wet-toed to the spring
for mam's tea: spam on Sundays
and chips if there is coal.
In the Orient I would be a good servant
willing to please.
Damping of strings my speciality,
an hired mourner
for the rest of my days: gazer
at umbrellas and rain.
No use for owt else up here
except wiping my legs of heifer muck
and fetching the four o'clock milk.
In the byre alone I weep

at the imagined contrivance
of straps and wires
locking my loll-tongue gargoyle head.
My muzzle gushes rain
and I wince when people speak to mam,
giving me their sideways look.
My eyes go furious and I stamp, stamp, stamp.
Pulse fever even in Hartfell sleet.
Loud tumult, what there is of my mind
tumbled into the lashing trees. Yes,
I love falling, caught momentarily
through each tall command of branches, amazed once more
at the borage blue sky
in another September afternoon
with tongue spouting, soaking the cones, thudding
to the very ground, disturbing
all the birds and worms and wasps and bees.
Don't count on me for fun
among the towering cowslips,
but please don't crush my heart.

Billy Mills

Ballad: Of Motion

one   two
me   you

      *

walking the same way daily
insensate ritual delight
in motion   words signs
the centre escape me

mind invents structure
in fog on the downs
accents our isolation
ambiguous fallacies

outward & home
the small book of nature
explained these consequences
our difficult future

      *

flying westward son
colouring rainbow fish
textural criticism
familiar fields random

mosaic descend again
rain echoes comparative
history of feeling   song
words echo mind's music

in canonical order
defining silence
a syntax suspended (verb)
the space between

       *

one   two
me   you
breast   bone

       *

start here notice
abnormal traces wind
leaves brittle memories
uncertain persuasion

waiting to move time
(conditionally) onwards
impossible voices question
connections stagnant sleep

a space (you have seen it)
ergative verbs
the same event
dispersed perspectives

       *

knowing you don't know
road curves over
the bridge canal
& railway below

into the village
(a holiday) we have
come & are leaving
purchase

a family ticket
these silent mornings
comparison:
the art of memory

       *

fire   home
   water

*

proportion is everything:
tower & square
rhyme an instinct
the ideal city

a single memory
internalized
streets necessary
the garden shimmers

step in the river
feel stability
& flux   words bend
under such pressure

*

night gathers line
forms this darkness
sit at the table
(genetic imperative)

naming the sound
time polyvalent
energy the core
vocabulary light

dims heat settles
presentation cephalic an-
terior we have been here
too long

*

one   two
me   you
breast   bone
fire   home
          water

Geraldine Monk

CS

Cirrostratus
smooth   subdued
still kinda whitish
but veiled
            partially
sometimes   or   sometimes
            totally

transparent overcast
breeding
kinda whitish rimmed
haloes
spiralling down to
consumptive rouge
with bits of seethe and brood
very low keyed rage

another step in depression sequence

last and empty pkt under footcrush

approaching rain
promising small insects walkies
on water

AC

Altocumulus
bragging shadow plus
big scaled
thickness
white bowing out now
                reluctant

haloes
invert to coronas
           red rimmed
eyes sting on smoke and
light wave
           trigger
of greenness
impressing many dreams touched
sour
aristocratically hung till
maggoty
or more commonly till hungering layers
of shading weigh humourless
rolling memories / cigarettes / clouds
which may / may not
be merged

South Bound: Facing North

Out of tube and tune
buskers   riff
rolling would-be saints and
                    soldiers sweat.
(Stiff and prickly's the smell of it)

Such warmth is uncouth
Such warmth leads to
      sibilants—
the thick hiss and prodding fingers
of sun and subways
                    long
           and burn for damp bronchial skies.

Listen: on the downwind
           wheezing amphibians
           fuff   fuff   fuff
wet-glass-hoppers
crawl and cluck
           cluck opinions
from flat and misspelt eyes
                         panning

and panting
jangled chords of
mischief dealt
fair and tenderly across its
broken bottle landscape.
                    Iced
                    Glint
                    and
                    Wink

La Tormenta

(with plundering of The Tempest)

Heat that feb ice. Spell melt.
T'wild frozen waters in that
ittered sky pelt downd
sunless pitch
jagged — it pricks the
soft cheeky brains. Afeard minds.

S'long Inglaterra. S'long Orchard Square.
Us runaway names about to
be cast stoneyed taxing down
the airy all ways of eternity.

                    *

upslung at last orgasmic gasp
hook off nerves
stripped bare eyes
leaking see-through pollen.
Sighing. It's true is that.
What! Must our mouths be cold?

(you are young you said you must enjoy your
self
your self who died beyond
the nine lives of cats)

Sprit guide riding high. Mischef meker.

Not half-drunk enough. Not half-love.
Even when an hourish later
paprika earth hit us at a half slant
dazzling unexpect of spice
heating hot
appalling hungers for
everything but food.

Cravedaze. Not half.
Half-not cut. Enough.
Rubbed crumpled eyelids
seez duty freez vanish.
Who put wild water in this roar?

An unsettled fancy is upon us.
An unwrit score rewritten.
'Fasten your seat belts' says Bette,
at the foot of the bumpy stairs.

With flick o wrist
t'heavens
opened.

Sonic bullroarers
neckbreakers
stampeders
on the wing
shaking living daylights
oust our dreading bones.
Toss't dice. Vinegar.

Fly blowing. Hoisted.

We split we split farewell!

(tricksy spirits were abroad)

Down
and out in
sting of godglitz
weighted with static collective
thanking sighs.

Tongue tips kiss
grit and tracery of dog
shit soft staining drinks
stick to lips—cling film—cling
filigree of dead skin
glitter dust of fag ash
cheek to check
signature of some body's blood
drip-written on pave stones

terror terra firma · WONDEROUS HEAVY

Eric Mottram

Elegy 11: Ford

for Lee Harwood

        one dread knocked out another
poverty   insults   punishments
incredible shyness   betrayals
            a creature of dreads
            taken prisoner
in contaminated fields
                an inviolable corner
                        vision
          simulacrum
    no lease
as if breath were amplified   spread in the air

a temporary respite from friends from destiny
     a proposition
             assured nooks houses that never cowered
        some Bemerton
   after their hard labours of engrossment and serenity
   work as work a garden to make fine
   marrows large as barrels
   a poem as beautiful as independent

a delight to watch two cats race in an old lilac
"they lived in the air whilst we plodded amongst mud and barbed wire"

        you come to the door
        there is no enemy
     threshold of noise shifts but never to silence
     clairaudience declines sounds cake a world
       saturated in isolation
a manliness of withstood din at the production line
        in the racket of profit
        deafens each worker inward
          quiet is forbidden music censored by amplification
          sounds push up his nostrils

lungs dream unmediated wind at a cliff edge

we came to a white sand   village underswept by tides
quiet offshore fishing prows and sterns upcurved
beyond number   women painted dyes in waxed cloth
       blue from sky and sea
       orange and brown from fruit and earth
dogs and cats in house ladders   giant lily nets flung on blue surfaces
houses of tied wood and palmetto thatch   a place whose patience
slowed through a night constellated in silent resin burners
     phosphorous ripples
     laughter of naked bathers
                  under a star blaze
     pungencies through cool airs
            a brief unseen presence
            unknown flowers take the senses
 a brief moonlight high
            there is the horizon and there
            outline
 patience a giant tree of rings
            a raft of tolerance
            a net to dream on flee from assail
   a vanished sanctuary
   a criticism of tolerance
   a previous patient universe
   gone down some line

two blackheaded men with guns terrorize an assistant his wife and girl
a sanctuary of tight mask and butt kick   a smell of fired exhilaration
a four inch shell is loaded   your uniform next the breach
inside the casing of a kind of shelter   a logistic probability of dials
       a kind of accuracy

such men need the extinction of wars for works carried through
a concealed bay out of memory   any green field any bit of loyalty
an enraged meticulousness   when the Minister required him
to accept an honour   he asked for ferrets
he carried slit trench in his head   barbed hedge of protection
the men could rely on him   a path finder
treachery in him impossible   an early morning completion
from which a launching   is possible
after sleeping clarities

             is there then any

terrestial paradise

        whispering olives

                people whom they like
        have what they like
        take their ease
        in shadows and coolness
        to love growing shape
        place it on your hand
        toward

Zuni Dancers

"now it's time for me to go to my society
for I'm the one that holds the song string tonight"

they wear masks a string of small sleigh bells
around the waist   gobs of streaky orange clay over
the body fringed leggings red buckskin moccasins

his orange helmet mask of Hatoshuka   Laguna mudhead clown
each tiny knob filled with clay from the river bank
at Kachina Village   tied close with cotton string
ends with a fluffy turkey breast feather   two others in salmon-red
body paint with burnt yellow racing spots   sweet smelling
bandoliers of cedar berries   embroidered kilts red and green
woven sashes   another mask painted does bucks fawns
romp in a forest glade chase butterflies jump over rainbows

a mask of many flowering twigs meadow flowers humming birds
bumble bees butterflies land feed take off

both masks have dragonflies and tadpoles flying swimming
up the back   song upon song overlap with rattled dew claws
on turtle shells waterpools of sound crossed by lightning rod
rattles cowbells pulsed pottery drums

medicine men call in beast priests and game animals
from their six directions   north south east west zenith nadir

clowns yell out masked dancers push their words through

long leather teeth lacquer red tongues

"a man who wears a mask should follow the rules
sobriety sexual continence   drunk or promiscuous
his mask may choke him to death or stick to his face
change him over into a dead person"

"his mind must be blank so that the mask
cannot control him"

permanent masks kept in sealed pottery jars in private homes
fed at each meal by the house-owner
if a man die without a personal mask he cannot return
from Kachina Village to dance with his group

mask appears before sleep or at waking control dreams between
since it can smother a man must sacrifice food pray to it:
                now we shall live together
                one another as father

                do not be vindictive with me
                be sure to do as I have said

                now stand before me
                ask for my long life

"in this performance you do not become one
you imitate impersonate you step inside
you make it come alive make him a living
dancing singer you will become part but your body
will be the same but just the head you know your mind"

maskers bring life in the form of babies
crops riches health to Zuni from Whispering Water
Lake of the Dead just above Kachina Village

"also cure fear anger rheumatism pneumonia other ailments
most dance songs speak of corn fulfilment of promises
reaching of old age songs especially healthy for the depressed
who feel they may just die"

but mudhead clowns funny dangerous are children of ancient

brother and sister incest penises tied playing silly begging
through the village around dancers hard to believe
to deny them anything even in one's mind attracts violent death

    half naked dirty in raggy black blankets
    loin cloths kilts these mean clowns
    wait like ravens like vultures

Wendy Mulford

Nevrazumitelny

To Mary Butts (1890–1937)

A letter like pink thrift breaks up the rock-slate
& glasses reach into intimacy I see you I see
through you intimately in an unfinished pose like
Degas precipitately over your shoulder slightly
dematerialised

The image of beauty of black limousine fetichism
keeps you fastened to the face toe by toe
juddering the musculature these spy-glasses
tracking the optic in which I see you composed
when the picture is finished the subject comes
back

The rock faults risk at the edge long ago
Christmas curtains collecting points wash away
evasiveness enters puckering the flesh small
pieces lost small losses pieced all the way
from yesterday for an artist time can always be regained
in the luxury of disarray

Six rocks
six lumps of quartz from the dismembered mine
at Botallack the light failed in winter working
reworking the rock the
crystalline quartz seamed with granite their flesh
& blood dis-eased mis-used former profit
forgotten sweat & blood sewed stony
tracings brief & witty at the end of a year of labour
come off it

Air and sea slap us surround the sneaking sea-mist
trance shush withdrawing particular moments of
great pleasure & great pain chisel the rock pretty
colour the curious claws of the spectator

Rocks & hollows
cliff-face marram-grass hoping
eroding land you are smoothed
worn hollow
bluntly wrapped is drifting

Button your flies
loosen your tie
sinking down
current eddying a
rock gull
hovering mid-air
face to face
you are enclosed in this frame
to which you are working
making this space and

self & self
brevity sings

I dreamt delicacy
in dark undertones

my flesh lacily edged
with capture

breaking the frame
the poem reaches for the gun

reserved hauteur
glances reserved

hauteur retreat

So there went your life
person to person
running wild again

> your legs shake your throat
> winds tremble
> gulls gouge out those eyes

> at the end of the year
> time on the rocks
> ragged rascals run on
> jagged paschal
> pink & creamy
> ribboned hearts
> glittering & wondering

> the silk the rose the quartz
> behind glass keepsake
> any line you don't buy

Grace Nichols

Long-Man

(For Barbara Cole who first introduced us to the Long-Man
For Jan and Tim who came along
And to The Druid Way *by Philip Carr-Gomm)*

On open downland we're as open as he—
Me and Jan, Tim and John,
Kalera and Ayesha,
And the cracked-sun
Has once again withdrawn.
Leaving us to windy shawls
And pewtery greys
To newly mowed down
Fecund-earth which the rains
Had furrowed into clay.

Plod-Plod
Through the caking-blood
Of England's sod,
Our good shoes growing
Sulkier by the minute,
As is my five-year-old,
Whose hand a sixth sense
Tells me to hold,
Despite her intermittent tugging
On this our hill-god pilgrimage.

And even when she manages
To break free, I'm after her,
A wiser Demeter—
Swiftfooted and heavy
With apprehension.
Sensing the weald-spirits
In a primitive pull
Of the pagan dimension.

'We're off to see
The Long-Man, the wonderful
Long-Man of Wilmington,'
I sing, humouring her over
The timeless witchery
Of the landscape.

Meanwhile, as always, he's there,
Looming out of the green coombe
Of Windover's womb.

In our heart-searching
And soul-yearning
We come to stand before him,
But soon our luminous eyes
Are nailing him with a
Crucifixion of questions—
Who and Why and How he came to be.
Male, Female, or ancient
Presage of a new androgyny?

With the sun back out
Surely he is benevolent
Corn-God and Shepherd
Of the good harvest?

Sun-in and he's
The Phantom-Symbol
Of all our foreboding.
The Gatekeeper-Reaper
Who would reap us in.
The faceless frozen traveller.
Moongazer.
Green Man-Mirror,
Tricking our eyeballs on—
The cunning chameleon.

But going back over
The wet green swelling
The presumptuous Goddess in me
Looks back and catches him—
Off guard.

Poor wounded man,
The staves in his arms
No barrier to a woman like
She-who-would-break-them
And take him in her arms.

Black

Show me the woman
that would surrender
her little black dress
to a white-robed clan
and I would show you a liar.

Not for their bonfire,
her wardrobe saviour
the number
in which she comes
into her own power.

Go to a funeral
in black and know
that the dead
beside the white candles
will not be offended.

Add amber earrings,
perhaps a hat or scarf of pink
and know you are ready—
for a wedding.
How black absorbs everything.

Stand around at a party
in black—you are your own artist,
your own sensual catalyst,
surprised to say the least
when black brings you

Those sudden inexplicable hostile glances.

White

Never mind how or why—
this slow delight
of waking to a room
that comes out of the
memory of night,
A dusky dawning—
paintings, wardrobe,
hangings . . .

Then walking, a sleepwalker,
holding on to walls of vanilla,
great solid slabs
you could sink your mouth into.
The memories of ancestors,
all that blackness
against whiteness.
The starched religiousness of it.

O I could hold
the globe like a face,
Januslike spinning
from the depths of my dreaming
I could face-up
to the stark white page
already seeded
with the best invisible poem.

Douglas Oliver

The Oracle of the Drowned

Memory in sea-green with sea-weed grain
of glass as the rearing wave rains briefly
before a lot of bother
on the beach of childhood
and men with a burden file across sand.
Those far-out surfaces are lipped
with transparent phrases coming to mind:
that the real dying happened in middle heights
between the lips and the sea floor.
Remember the swim trunks lost in waters
and the first man in our lives who drowned,
this, now, his cortege from the tide-edge,
the sacred hanging-down of head and arms
seeing that person's white groin
cooked chicken bared near the hook of the ribs
and a shore-line of horrified children
arrested in their digging to gaze
at seas of such corruption as to change him.
His shirt left behind too long on the promenade rail,
always there in our lives, its caked cotton
fluffy-white in its inner wrappings.
The cloth wandered open at nights as we wondered
what a drowning body could say
when its chest became translucent green,
we courted in our minds such corrupt purity,
never escaping but sinking into not
the unthinkable gift of the self to death,
not the sea flash flood in the throat,
but into the oracle of the drowned;
because the oracle of the dying comes to a halt
but the oracle of the dead continues and has humour in it.
We ask the dying, 'How do you go about drowning?'
and the answer comes first 'I cannot—'

then swims in ambivalent vowels
and voiceless consonants in the washing tide
voiced consonants in the last buzz of the eardrum:
'Aah, I am funtoosh, zooid, walway,
wallowing, rows and rows of waves,
a goooood one, my soooul a sea-mew' —
and we learn nothing but the knowledge of pain,
and the hope of a future from it.
But the gone-dead are beamish and talk to us
from out of memory's hollows and gulphs:
'You, boy, in your Bournemouth bed, be with me now
and I will come to you many years later
still drowned in a medium of green liquid
the water whispering through its lips
as the dark whispers to you in caves or before sleep.
And I was a man and had babies
as you, a baby, will have a man and call him "Father"
and as the drowned will have the drowned.'

"u", "je", "r", "r", "im", "a", "finally"

What does the "u" mean in "gradual"?
and "je" in "Betjeman"?
the second "r" in "hero"?
and the second "r" in "parricide"?
What does the "im" in "imperfect" mean?
What does the letter "a" dog do?
What do you mean, "finally"?

Answers: "Gradual" is the slave of the letter "u".
          "je" is not here the French for "I"; however, it is the point of
              individuality in "Betjeman".
          The second "r" is the hero, wounded, still with labours to perform.
          The second "r" is hand-mixture, twist, a long line forwards.
          The "im" means nothing is so imperfect it is not already perfect.
          The dog jumps on the letter "a" until his footprints are all over the
              paper and he can't see the letter "a". Then he wonders why he
              keeps on jumping on it.
          What do you mean, "finally"?

A Little Night

A word to come lies in a little night
where ash is falling.
The word can't be this "coffin,"
lying in its candour, in its cinders.
Inside, the poet's too lazy in his death
to perform a truth singly. All's ambiguous.

Yet a coffin is blocked in boldly, I see,
under the washing down of night.
The cobalt blue cabinet's cut on a slant
with candlelabra making mirrors
along its sides peopling it with mourners,
delegates from the governments of poetry
and from their industries, who appear
only as reflections of shoulders.
Hostility of moths round the candles.
Hostility of mouths still saying "coffin."

The coffin waits in this little night
for the whole day's train.

My own face, visible in the mirrors now,
is a bruise again floating in hints of crystal.
I don't *yearn* towards my shadow, bowing
to it, reaching out to find lost unity;
for if the shadow really touched my finger
untruth would constitute truth, whereas
as Buber knew, the process takes a *Thou*.

Our shadows lack performance;
they are a text created by the dusty mirror:
I do all the touching and my finger
returns with its ashen tip, as you
the reader, when you touch these unreal ashes
find your own finger-tip is clean.

In our candour to be truthful, we're very stern
and talk too much of loss, covering our truths
with ashes—like authoritarian fathers
who damn their sons with an over-strict word,
"You'll never amount to anything."

The word I care about
(it's been lying inside the slant cabinet)
wakes and now performs itself.
The word becomes "Celan," formerly "Antschel":
the only poet I have to struggle against
because none wrote more beautifully post-war
of the perfection and terror of crystal.

Walnut and Lily

> And even if rose and nightingale
> were fabricating what they feel, it would have
> some benefit, as so often befalls.
> —HEINE, *Neue Gedicht*

White undervest nestling on black trousers
creeping round the bookcase in dawn light
seen before getting up to make coffee,
sad water lily under a love-pained moon.

That was said while tucking in a shirt,
a Heine piece of beautiful shit, said in thuds
for I keeled over dying on the floored mattress.
Nearly as bad as, "the void, the silence, the space
inside the word," a crock, this time, of shit
at a Celan conference—might as well crack open
walnuts with their diploid kernels, or set walnut
words bobbing about on a lake in a lyric,
ripples with narrow paddles of moonlight in hollows.

A breakfast sparrow chirps. Choosing a jacket,
I seem to have only two choices these days,
not the old romantic tweed but middle-age black
and Celanian gloom: I worry about Britain fallen
to gnawing its kernel. Today, a middle-class tie,
a nutty shade, honouring those architectonic
word knots of Celan, little tie nuts. *Die nachtigall!*

No Heine nightingales in Paris. Still half-dreaming,
I'm by a lake rescuing walnuts from the flood
(just a few last cornflakes in the bowl) and am

obscurely angry. Suppose our words cracked open
to another kind of light, not 'white void';
crack open Celan's hard-worn 'thought scarab';
crack open 'animal-bloodblooming';
crack open 'net-nerved skyleaf.'

See the walnuts in my dream-lake
rippling along like turds in creaming dawn,
or imagine a black scarab floating there,
make its carapace bloom with a lily.
Lift a precious walnut from out the waters,
thumb its wet shell open. Don't kid me, you don't
find silence inside but red heat, a tiny furnace.

Instead of that well-gnawed British despair,
instead of return to a middle-class Parnassus,
these words are angry, in a flood of lyric feeling:
I return the black jacket, put on the frayed tweed,
replace the tie, still knotted, in the cupboard.

Maggie O'Sullivan

A Lesson from the Cockerel

POPPY THANE. PENDLE DUST. BOLDO SACHET GAUDLES
GIVE GINGER. GIVE INK. SMUDGE JEEDELA LEAVINGS,
TWITCH JULCE. WORSEN. WRIST DRIP. SKINDA. JANDLE.
                   UDDER DIADEMS INTERLUCE.
                   ICYCLE OPALINE RONDA.
CRIMINAL   CRAB RATTLES ON THE LUTE.
CONSTITUENTS   BLINDINGLY RAZOR-GUT.
                   SHOOKER– GREENEY CRIMSON
                   NEAPTIDE COMMON PEAKS IN THE
                   SWIFT PULLERY. TWAIL,
                   HOYA METHODS: SAXA ANGLAISE
SKEWERED SKULL INULA.

2nd Lesson from the Cockerel

RIVERCRAFT. CAREY NEON. DOVE-WEBBING FATIGUES.
THE SASHED, SILENT ONE WHO HEARS. THEN AS ONE WHO.
CONJURING SPAT LIGHTS ON THE PALATE. MUSEY TIGHT
SADDED, HAWDY KERDY'S, RAGE RUGGING JET. PORTAGE
                   THICKENS (NERVINE SPARROWS IN
                   THE MOUTH BLISTER). RED STROUDERS
RIGHT-HAND   DEW-BUCKLING WINTER, TONGUE-A-SAD-
PASSAGEWORK   OF-ALL-BIRDS WHEN THE WAVES COME
                   BONED, BLEED LICKS THE SWIRE-HEAD.
                   THE DONE-SKIRT. THE SCALDING.
                   THE SHOT-OVER BELLIES READ WITH
                   JASPER, MINCE, THE MASSIVE SHIVERS,
                   LOOF, SWOLE: JUTTING MULTIPLICATION.

Narrative Charm for Ibbotroyd

Cobble & Pebble in the teeth. Fang & Club upon
a wind is the morning Fields Louded Ably Thus.

Snow of Earth bladder waking to a new Ear
when the stir of all Breath would to a Seeing turn,
wondered upon; housed many, unhurt is.

O, many berries, Occupying (& not), a Quarter-Day
heathered with Rawley Land of animal drumming many
gentled adjoining utterances.

Just as water does, between worlds, Giant eveyRUE BETHS here
edge the word. Crow trembles in the knot.

Hill Figures

nailed Eagles   beryl   alter vasish
   Owls, Blood-bed
   Bird-gear   turbulent

Ruled

it,

Raven

      blue acquiescing tar
          thread
   the.air.it.will.be.tinned.
          pull—
      feather against call—

Crow-Shade
plumb, true

        hemispheres
     (dwell-juggling)

          has shells,
          fan
          to
          resist—

Skull—

     a large, Oth
          Twisted

      merry-go

    superates,
congregates,

       rolled-a-run

       lettering

     Autistic low
      twindom

   to live in the Sky

to live Underground

Eagerly
as little names of both, Cow, horned to begin
        Horned to grow new

            skinning torso
            tinning lengths

            fin-

            bred-

                    Brinks

            Bladder-on-Stick

                    hand-in, hand-outa, hand—

        sacri
        DOSAGES
        invert
        reversionary
        morrow.

Giant Yellow

Intoothed Constrict

                    STRUT figure white many downwards,
                            anciently
                        ULTRA flutterings, how paper & swan

        made is

                    Eyes, Tongue, Jaw—

        craft / bodies
        Eagle's Bone

brine dyed
black
lasted
addly
surges

CLAW—

zipped differ
zephyr leaning to plight,
Cordoned, Colap
Bleeding

DRAKE'S FLIGHT
FOOL'S PAGE—

Median Sagittal Plain
Salts Mirror
Outer Poises Opaler Too.
Tear-low Slaughter
Steady on Horror
Crackly

Laddery

Triply Hooves
pounded stomach on string

Baffles
Abbreved
Gill-Breaths

JAMBREAK

foetal Mixey Hiss

Mixey

Field, The Casting Out of

collie dog pearls, purslane diarying

delete, DESIRED

Lipreads
Indigo Slips Reversing
Lateral
Sinuses,

mouse ear
earth
paraded
Grips dumbed
clutched

Arrow Inflorescence

Trance
Orbiting
2 Horns, scalded, misspelt. Approximal
membraneous shadow plaiting, the
Letter Missing, Missingly

Climates end, Spans—

of the Jar, Want Conductors, Want Light—
Want as a Province of sheer Retinal Directory—

"memories are made
made of this are"

Embryonic lassing
ARTILLERY

Crosses. Crisscross, Crossings gone
Carapace
Cutaway Iambic
Cloaca documents, Octaves of the Kidney

the grave has never been

fleeing
it possesses
in the hollow of trees
in return
of blue
of nuts
its long sleep

arrested

                        *

A pen ticks,
Body of the Animal Altered
HELD

DREW

A coast thumps, flank of a Corpse —
(Collapsed
Only Bigger —

BORN.

Meso-cysted
BELLOW geometries

Oxidised
Dalliances —
chain-blue

KID-EYED ICER BARS—

So go,

Purpleda Down. Pursea. Vents Trembling

THORNSWAY SINGINGS

in a cyclic manner—
in mammalian muscle—

So gather,

(dock & sorrow
totems—
Rickety Hooley Stutter—

Spine
slub

Squabble-Speak
sub—

statuary—

(a tentative of ease), Gived Contortionist:

Sylla/

      bled Garjey,

auric   fin   spun   key   skins
Boundary between

                        —Twilight Powders

                        —The Pulse in Health

—acro   pleural   petal   fugal
—thick   fat   spat   fast

whenas crack
& hammer—

drumming juniper lids

a drum
a drum

RAVEN
it is
touched it

                    shimmer gifts meant
                        hoofmarks
                      hairsbreadth

                    Winged Antimony
                       Entered
                    Lacerations
                         Risen
              Earth tr, Yellow Tooks

        birds & their habits—jump the channels

              call the visions in

Tom Pickard

The Devil's Destroying Angel Exploded

     no sound
but horns of Southern ships
       and flapping wings

no colour
      but dancing black

producers of heat
      confused in the cold

moon full above the dole

     sleep children of chilled night
whose fathers were black men

     sleep bairns, shiver now
ya fathers' gold is stolen

     strong fathers of a harsh past
     despondent now
slag faces rot against the dole

your hands held hammers
     & demanded much
the moment passed
     bairns curled cad in the womb

     you worried troops and churches
suffocated in the Durham bishop's stables
     when Londonderry's jails were full

     the coal you hewed
should have burnt them alive
instead you begged another shilling

you should have thrown it
in their faces like a bomb
        fed your children joyful stories
                of the blood of those
        who cheat us

        where we live
shattered smiles
        break on haggard faces

        manufacturers of filth
marry our wealth
        in a confetti of votes

no breath of slum air

councillor, elected by my father,
        he said you wore a worker's cap
called everybody *marra*
        the word I heard was slave

bloodfluke in the brain of an ant
        that gold chain scraped
from the lungs of pitmen

your gown is a union leader
        gutted and reversed

        look dozy fathers look
your masters have changed
        drawn by the rivermist
you drift in a dream

ah father, your flesh is overrun with lice
and all your life you nurtured many parasites

Bush Telegram

bird chase bird
        through thicket leaves

we'll make love
    where earth bleeds

bird chase bird
    on desert sand
we'll make love
    in no man's land

bird chase bird
    on mountain sides
we'll make love
    where water divides

bird chase bird
    beneath a fern
we'll make love
    beside a burn

bird chase bird
    through burning grass
we'll make love
    and dance and laugh

bird chase bird
    from dawn to dusk
we'll make love
    till love makes us

What Maks Makems

an icy wind bites
    through stocks
whipped-up
    from the Wear
  where shags in a frozen
    dive
break black water

  a crick-neck welder
bent
  beneath the boat

with his head in a mask
　　burns her together

　　he crawls
　　in a double bottom gutter
beneath the engine room
　　tank-top
to the sump
　　where the clatter
　　　and rattle of caulkers
shatter the ear
　　drum running shudder
of a bulkhead drop

　　the only way out
in a panic
is backwards
over
　　an extractor pipe
and cables
　　through a hatch
　　　got smaller
in a swollen flap

the Makem can
　　weld himself into
　　　a steel box
and seal the lid on
　　afterwards

Makems: Wearside shipbuilders

mY peN

holds steady in my right hand
black, with a silver top
and tight gold nib

my **hero pen**
made in the People's Republic of China

and purchased in Warszawa
by my wild, cloud-haired, Polish wife
with apple-green eyes
and twenty faces

my **hero pen**
joins vertical strokes
to curved and looping horizontals
sucks noisy and quick
when dipped in black India ink

my **hero pen**
speaks slim volumes
running its incised beak
along prescribed lines

my **hero pen**
feels good between
finger and thumb

my **hero pen**
purchased in Dom Ksiazki,
on Nowy Swiat
where walls of books
are dripping ink
and threaten to flood whole streets

my ebony black, silver topped
Golden Star, Seven O Five
Chinese **hero pen**
looks good
with a blue and chrome
Three Seven One
YEUN CHANG—
made in Changhai,
comma,
China—
best quality,
swivel-type stapler
with four different uses

my pen writes adverts
for its comrades

my pen shouldn't get
too smart

My pen's ink
is the distilled dream
of fifty thousand million workers
weary with clocking-in
and clocking-out,
signing-on
and signing off:
enslaved to machinery
of industry
and state.

my pen refuses to recognise
obsolete forms of government
and votes with its feet

my pen wants to manage
its own affairs
thinking it knows best:

my pen demands
complete autonomy

Elaine Randell

from *Songs for the Sleepless*

"You were too busy being. And you are too busy now. You couldn't spare the time to note down a few facts: how the sun and silence poured into the big room with the yellow curtains; how everything was never ending and expendable."

ELIZABETH SMART

Tomorrow I shall.
Tomorrow time will be used as soap, to be spread
cleansed with.
Crying spells.
Perhaps soon the day will be an agonising howl
as the Donkey in the next field screams out at all human suffering
and ceaseless need.
I have almost given up hope of using the moment for that which it is
to take in sensually the second the open heart the open heart.

"The cheap Sparrows peck about in the dust."

ELIZABETH SMART

What else is there to do
but to go after a special index of passion.
Praise the long limbs of young men
and the downy hair on their brown forearms
and the edges of fresh white shirts
covering the sides of strong capable chests.
Knowing becomes loving.
It's not who you are but whose you are.
Local means safe means close.
On the motorway Sparrowhawks loom over litter
bins and foreign trucks pass on the inside lane.

I can't settle this
I can't sleep.

Hard To Place

I

His mother, a petrol pump attendant, was said by those who knew her to be far less than bright. She had not wanted the child but had wanted his father. She grew very fat with the pregnancy but told no one of the forthcoming child inside her. On the forecourt of the garage she went into labour while delivering three gallons of four star. They stifled her screams with the rag that wiped the dip stick and mopped her waters with the sponge that cleaned the windscreens.

Now eight years later he's a tiny child and the doctors write notes about his small head circumference and his stammer. He has moved eight times in the last three years, he is a difficult boy. The woman from the home writes on his review form that he often uses situations to his own advantage. His gait is odd, she comments, and he frequently limps to attract the attention of adults.

II

Late one January night when the whole house was sleeping the young mother put her careful plans into action and slipped away from her family and its life. The three tiny children remained asleep until 7am and their father until 9. It has long been agreed that the woman has returned to Ireland and all efforts to trace her through the newspapers, police and Salvation Army have now been terminated. When the children realised their mother had gone they tried to ring her on their toy telephones and sent her letters through the Mr Men post office. They cried themselves to sleep most nights and have been constantly greedy for food.

When their father realised his wife had gone he spent the family allowance at the bookies and told the welfare that something would have to be done. He signed them into care and jumped beneath the Northern Line on the way home. It is true to say that the children with their 6, 4 and 2 years are a handful and tend to be clingy. Only last week the eldest boy was found asking a policeman to please find his mummy.

III

It had all been too much one way and another. The fact that her boyfriend had been taken away in a police car that morning, her final demand from the credit card company had been delivered, the flat reeked of the damp and the child was fretful. She collected together her purse, pushchair and raincoat and set off for the shopping precinct. Once inside she felt better but the child moaned for sweets and the piped music mixed with the lights and her lack of food made her become dizzy. Sitting down next to an elderly couple who were rearranging their shopping, she enquired whether they would keep an eye on the child while she found a toilet. Two hours later the couple continued with their attempt to extract information from the wailing child. Eventually the precinct security guard took the child away and a police woman was called. The sobbing of the infant drowned even the piped music.

Now, four years later, the little girl has a new family who worry about her insecurity and dreadful fear of open spaces.

IV

After her brother had been killed by swallowing the bleach she came into care. Her mother had asked that she be taken away before she harmed her. The last she saw of her mother was never to be forgotten, she has no recollection of her father at all but it is believed he works on a fairground. She frequently has terrible nightmares that wake the whole home. The staff say she encourages boys to come into her room, she has absconded on two occasions when the fair has been in town.

Her mother is now in prison and she has written to her but has received no reply.

The staff at the home would like her to live in a family to be taught some discipline since everyone believes she is promiscuous and could be in moral danger. She is nine years old and calls her dolly 'Mummy'.

The Snoad Hill Poems

for Ian

1

O house, O sloping field, O Poplar trees whose tall arms salute.
Bleating
Bleating everything is looking.   The cows call
                                    at night
                                    for their calves
                                    removed after
                                    weaning. Four
                                    days later they

give up
throats sore.

I am at a loss to cleverly describe the lights
from the tiny train in the distance snaking its way
south from London across the Kent land.
"A necklette of tynie golden stones or
a worm of saffron slipping through a lanyard of light."

2

Walking towards the village
the moon as bright as a cats eye
thin film of cloud across the empty
autumn fields.
I am wondering you see about this
thing they call chance . . . .

How it was that you and I became this way
we hadn't noticed the sun lifting the
trees upward . . . . . so much power in the trunk.

The way we've chosen to arrange ourselves.
The tired manner of the chin of an
old person standing watching
goes up and down
seen it all before worn out.
Why are we always moving about?

3

She had the stance of a Snowdrop.
It concerned him that already the wind had
been exposed to her face and that her
lightly chapped skin made an embarrassed glance
appear on her face. Perhaps it was all the crying
that wet her face.
The womans countenance was bright and her
unusually welcoming manner was renowned.
"It was always thus" she said to him late
one afternoon as he packed the car "always it
is the woman who waits and says little."
Glancing back as he drove away he caught her

eye in the rear view mirror and was reminded
of the first day he had seen her.
The air had been warm during the night and the
next day he had set off to town to buy
an extractor fan. She had been standing across the
road talking to an older man, her hand
on his shoulder, her head in his hands.
He was struck then as now that she was as pale
and thin as a Snowdrop and that if she bent
any closer towards the earth she would simply
snap.

4

And if my light should
sudden peter out
do not grieve
thinking
I had not time to
admire the upturned leaves.
Just today
I brought home
Rose bay willow herb
Cow parsley and fern
Germander speedwell
and this mitre headed beauty
is bright yellow Kidney vetch.
What more can you hope for.

5

Digging up weeds by the little hedge
the spade hits the store of Bethersden
marble that is the foundation here.
13th century clay threw up Palidisa Carnifera
composed almost totally of fresh water snail
fossilised.
Cut and polished   so striking
Cranbrook and Biddenden pavements show the
pock marked broken down snail shells.
Cut and polished   so striking are
the Cathedral and nave steps in Canterbury
and Rochester, the Great West tower of

Tenterden church.   In the buildings of
Woodchurch and Headcorn and Hythe the finest
examples are found, the best seen of its value.

Pale and dark brown and blue almost luminous tints
feel alive when touched.
Gentle water snails skate in the dykes.
"It bears a good polish and is very hard
and durable if dug up in its perpendicular
state but if horizontally found it peels off in flakes."

Ox drawn sledges dragged these great marble
slabs to surrounding villages and to the lodges
of the masons who worked it.

6

Our hands crushed
bent back against one another
we turn for warmth and find only dampness rising
from our troubled palms as if
all Cyprus trees were in troubled prayer.
The tiny branches and new shut buds of our unborn child
lay alert listening to the dark damp womb.
Walking out along Sparrow Hatch lane the exquisite woodsmoke
no moon but the sharp light from the London train
coming home South.
An alarmed creature in the hedgerow, turns round, sees me
and takes off.

7

Its this familiar black line from the tops
of the trees making their way up to the woods
from the edge of the field.
Near the small white bridge the cows move off.
Late Harvesters come home after dark
tractor and trailer lights blazing as they pass.
Inside me
you my first born move with such force, pushing organs into your own
shape. Coming to us, as you do, with nothing. I too have nothing
but these arms to offer and this heart from which you take   life,
this comfort for always yours.

ELAINE RANDELL   195

8

Waiting
all of us
the Jersey cow and her smooth red body swollen
tight with calf. Long tongue sucking up grass,
conkers hang
some darker than others, always they seem too early.
Acorns tiny in their cups rattle in the air.
Ease. Grace. I am won over and quite ready.

9

Temperament is related to physique.
Heavy showers on and off all day soaking
into the dry earth. The first rain in three weeks.
Turgid stems turn small flower faces skyward.
"Jesus wants me for a sunbeam" I know he does.
In Georges garden a white lilly has opened
up and made me think of him a week
before he died saying
"I'm so confused, I'm so old, it doesn't seem
at all right me being like this."

10

The jetty
just before Christmas
the whole bay out there and the little boats
in the frozen water.
How else can we sharpen our hearts on the first
bleat of morning from our small bed where we lay curled
together in sleep.
Your dark ginger curls on the pillow and the autumn
leaves under the car headlights
are at night the axis for all this living.

11

The hedge breaks out in bud
giving it that bullion coated tinge
we associate with frost.
Sparrows chip along looking to make nests

and the sheep lay close by too heavy with lamb.
"Why can't we go for walk and come back pleased"
The blackbirds glazed black body on the garden
post waxed against rain the sparklets of water
he shakes off before he sings before he flies.

Tom Raworth

Future Models May Have Infra-Red Sensors

take a taxi and go fishing
how do you like that?
visit canada
hey look, i see a big moose

cat's nose is twitching
why don't you ever go
to work and earn money?
invest your money here

why don't you try it yourself?
i'm on guard duty
with the armoured car
could you give me a lift?

then we could buy some lunch
gentlemen, here comes lunch
there is all the food we want
just give me a microsecond

maybe you likee something
to eat while you wait?
of course, of course, well, well
i'll prove it to you

you sir. who, me sir?
well sir, what is the verdict?
believe me
i've never seen my sheet

tell me again, i don't get it
sorry, hotee dogs all gone
a natural using wild game
one share of wildcat oil

don't cut *me*. i never
heard of wildcat oil
broken glass, drawn stars
fine, fine, you killed him

hold it officer, it's my duty
right behind the car sir
before anyone sees me
my pleasure, you know what they say

money talks. i just don't understand
xylophone trills
another day like yesterday
we'll be in gravy

pardon me gentlemen
is there a bank
in the neighbourhood?
you drove up from hillcrest?

That More Simple Natural Time Tone Distortion

slow
low
thump
long flame
dry
flash blur
just
move
tree browns
to south
our horse
white
no trace
of action
in memory
and fear
but this
is

clear
this area
this never
ending
song
to last
gasp
cold colours
enough
flashes
to leach him
out
as she
sparkles
that i will bear
two faces
and allegiance
mister cheap justice

bubbles
in
the silent
night
no control
over
extremities
bark
companion
words
twist off
what has
no name
salt
dragon
cartoon
cactus
close up
to empty
face
or back
of head
he could
be going
any
way
the presence
of nothing
slow
remember
food
this one
is still
grey
sound
stripes
layer
swift
so seal
of approval
leaves
no impression
see

possession
know
whimper
warm red
looks
at me
real
just went
by
late
again
slash
lights
diagonal
direction
of icy
moon
howl
scratch
soft knuckles
at the door
above
the tempo
flesh
tuner
shriek
right
we slide
out
into
filtered
footstep
mimic
ape
read
new
solids
not
pressed
prayer
aware
my brothers
we

for the love of
god
enter
spaces
of tradition
lean
far star
seen
atween
car
jar
keen
ears ending
tone
spheres
contending
alone
i love
empty
books
don't you
so
my awakened
spirit
weeps
i
can imagine
not imagining
that
STARTS
you
stay here
fall
in love
meet
mister
metaphor
shoot it
from cold
words
used out
give
space

TREMOR
TREMOR
stillness
of
my present
moves
within
me
chill sheets
chime
stained
ice
shatter
shadows out
without
falls
in
to memory
edmund
dante
caught
by a thought
nature
inclines
towards
risk
no
further
than you
can go
tempo
moon
my tube
moon
slow behind
silence
peace
or play the
game
i love
your music
muse
nor will

silence
slide
those fibres
of my love
for vanity
disfigures me
why cold
if ay
reflection

flames
to memory
games memory
of games
then silence
wakes me
with a
break
in waves

Dark Senses

bones show through images
of friends though they
still move in dialogue
in darkness what relief

forgive me, it's a dream
standing alone, waving
in search of its lost era
not just geography

walking parallel streets
of tropical flames
with a political broom
ominous as a smoke signal

over a farewell meal
of dust in the dust
before an open window
weather permitting

step sharply within
the labyrinth of raw meat
jingling those keys
dimmed by sweat

unthinking insects click, rustle
for bare subsistence
in the skeletons of organisations
inexorably crushed by vice

they themselves go into hiding
one on top of another
in their natural colours
green smocks, masks and goggles

taking likenesses
to build a screen
alongside the trail
of pearl lightbulb shards

this curiously shaped barrier
contains gestures and rites
simulated leopard skins
smart cards and our ideas

for fear of disturbing
the pose of philosophy
fashionable at the time
they stand in complete silence

in unbroken sunlight
wearing masks
as aids to memory
attributed to interiors unknown

they did not break
under their own weight
the experience of generations
proved far more effective

acts of representation respond
in order to survive desire
cheated by false hopes
in voices hardly above a whisper

local weather prophets
proclaim their laws of storm
radioactive rain restricted
to areas over toxic waste

the nightmare atmosphere of ruin
washes away in close-up
striking spatial effects predicted
if the mask is joyful

produce a sublime gesture
opposed to voice or action
a system of reflections ordering
the necessity of ornament

Out of a Sudden

(Riva san Vitale, August 30th 1995)

the alphabet wonders
what it should do
paper feels useless
colours lose hue

while all musical notes
perform only in blue

a lombardy poplar
shadows the ground
drifted with swansdown
muffling the sound

at the tip of the lake
of the road to the south

above in the night sky
scattered by chance
stars cease their motion
poppies don't dance

in the grass standing still
by the path no-one walks

Carlyle Reedy

The Doll Museum

    obsidian   sculpted lips slip
the unlit depth

              breath trapped
          narrow in apertures

Carved eyes watch
   the doll for movement

                  silence
               the catch

listen the rustle   fairy nets
tentative   lines by all exhibits.

furred oriental
Insect pulls rickshaw
thin leg line
under belly crawl

             toward a far oriental
           Longevity   Abacus
              fibular   fistula
                once was self
in a search for solutions,
at louis quinze set miniatures
our belief in a simple life
   pressed in mathematic
   back of chairs'
   shell, brush & mirror
Silver of moon spotted

floor, Owned floral
trusseau table, Watteau

Pressed muscle valvula
   thigh about to move
Walk on to the next face
   quivering its case
      the swift extinguisher
      or the fire too near.

in the glass a model is
        caught, it's registered
        1900 as "liebling,"
        closely in reflection
        fast shadow gathering
        a thought: "maybe death";
        yet model serenity
        vision 144
        alive in vapour touches
           our fog breath.

      small walnut
    open-skull empress,
tall, she's all beautiful,
each part fit   each slip
into side – inch centimetre
      finds
in a museum of crinolated dolls.

        breath abated by
             torn birds,
      feathers of blood,
   in drawn bellows poets wait to speak,
  to spark the dark to larksong then quiet.

sharp small teeth
   express the vicious
by strange bowing lamps;
   baffled are these faces
     placed amongst such treasures.

        example: 460 queen of else
        fears future; her eye
        lifts to cross waves,
        makes its ciphers of distress;
        her still sighs would express

memory, her sister, studding this doll woman.
clouds, loud and enormous, pass her.
      sculpted figure
      tat and parasol
      body of gold foil
      bead body Big
      spread in her sequins.

             example: monksbane
             nunhead at a millinery;
             or at the miller's some couple
             sadly religious.

           wolf on the tor plastic in forest
              faked pine   hide or lurk
                the beacon mind's light
                    in sudden swirl
               some leaves blown
                musty release from a blocked base
            & out of years' sleep

                open doors simultaneously
              turning the basil
          in a mouth of air a stick of sweet

              in anomaly of quiet
              wolf satiety
                the eaten silence.

good book one doll has heart held
Hell for that one interrupted eden
in high heat while her whole future slept
she was undone, briefly in some shadow
become a question as he was burned
      eyes staring where were
         his gods tarred in pitch

414 exhibit thick dark the test
    the way in —a proportional ticket
    the way out travelling an opposite direction
in bevelled geometry
                small sisters of Sky
             slide in the number seven

or in nought, in diminishing frame of whispered reference
        in desire to be other who is you as you do
ask questions of the other who asks too of you
        in a desire to be you continuance
            animate   in two lives of questions
                observations stagger   in the hushed museum.

Notes, from our museum of small victories
sketched displacement & accord of small faces
in a crowd we have created, for us, our voices:
sly poachers of endearing beatitudes
slip laughing tastes of crepe suzettes,
seem on the increase; our humanity sweats,
our intention is focussed: upon release
we get the histories out of the glass cases
& we free them — don't we — in our chaste respect
we do infuse   these dolls   with life ?

Sensuous Temples Body Houses
spaces so restless to meet their maker
sweet calls will fall into an odour
inhaled in gasses   flesh chemical
one day breaks to Orion
                            opens a strap
                        slips old striations
into night & night's disguises
in time
            to plummet
                        by inches to edge
a void at the measure
tape at the cases
        where the dolls do live.

120 up to nine
heads of pins
angle struck in
            light   threaded
                    firey filament
muses   the marvel
                death voodoo
        scars an instant   Terror exists
a body feels its sweating hand chasten
the waxen trap
                "let them out" cries blood.

the museum may be locked
the toys to crack
in suffocator cases
              unruled smoke
              spirit on the glass
fogs now to the last
Indian of porcelain.

              393 I'll take with me
              costing four fifty
              distribute to the country
              headless cotton stitch
              hidden clean stuffing;
dead in bed
388 the bed
unlisted numbers of golden bears
on pillows to children
all the size of thumbs with juices
pure as sweet fruit;

we're about to get out
yet fevered breath back of mean teeth
474 still waits, standing up
the giant wins his black cup.
the Museum cluttered,
bits of our flesh in its mortices,
the odd limb here or there
on a last shelf.

              437 sad
              cannot out loud
              patronize nor reject
              sticks in a gamesack
              nor a face stuck in kapok;

Merely nod, too slowly, the mechanical dog
clutches "save the animals" in one act
to live must abandon the dead
depart these digressions as the museum shuts
quick beneath the timed noises
    evoke the rare & exceptional

sailor woman
                    her bird green
sapling man
                    his feet earthed
direct the complex clothed & exhibited
dolls with plaster-busted shovels
dig now for treasure
                    each to each
speak in catalogue device
    unjustifiable in hope, awake
    In the breath of flesh
            fold/unfold
        in eyelet lace
                    the paper heart
                    the poets make.

Denise Riley

Lure, 1963

Navy near-black cut in with lemon, fruity bright lime green.
I roam around around around around acidic yellows, globe
oranges burning, slashed cream, huge scarlet flowing
anemones, barbaric pink singing, radiant weeping When
will I be loved? Flood, drag to papery long brushes
of deep violet, that's where it is, indigo, oh no, it's in
his kiss. Lime brilliance. Obsessive song. Ink tongues.
Black cascades trail and spatter darkly orange pools
toward washed lakes, whose welling rose and milk
beribboned pillars melt and sag, I'm just a crimson
kid that you won't date. Pear glow boys. Clean red.
Fluent grey green, pine, broad stinging blue rough
strips to make this floating space a burning place of
whitest shores, a wave out on the ocean could never
move that way, flower, swell, don't ever make her blue.
Oh yes I'm the great pretender. Red lays a stripe of darkest
green on dark. My need is such I pretend too much, I'm
wearing. And you're not listening to a word I say.

A Misremembered Lyric

A misremembered lyric: a soft catch of its song
whirrs in my throat. 'Something's gotta hold of my heart
tearing my' soul and my conscience apart, long after
presence is clean gone and leaves unfurnished no
shadow. Rain lyrics. Yes, then the rain lyrics fall.
I don't want absence to be this beautiful.
It shouldn't be; in fact I know it wasn't, while
'everything that consoles is false' is off the point—
you get no consolation anyway until your memory's
dead: or something never had gotten hold of
your heart in the first place, and that's the fear thought.
Do shrimps make good mothers? Yes they do.

There is no beauty out of loss; can't do it—
and once the falling rain starts on the upturned
leaves, and I listen to the rhythm of unhappy pleasure
what I hear is bossy death telling me which way to
go, what I see is a pool with an eye in it. Still let
me know. Looking for a brand-new start. Oh and never
notice yourself ever. As in life you don't.

from *Seven Strangely Exciting Lies*

i Take Two of These Tablets Tonight and in the Morning Go on Living

So get up speed. So you're sick with fear again so what so what
Though in the past you screamed you wept you are still here alive
Get up a head of speed and you may nip through rocks
                              without quite getting smashed apart on them
So you bit on iron until the blood ran out of your lips
So your eyes swam into dark blue clouds with the enormous misting shock of it
So you couldn't see your hands in front of you, you hardly knew how to breathe
yet you do take breath after breath, one by one you ease them all out carefully again
and then you take another, for someone else will tell you when it's time to stop, not you
So you ground your forehead onto the concrete to skin yourself back into manageable
      life
because a streak of dusty red showed you could start a little harm and stop and then
      restart it
but you lived it, look into your eye at the shiny black life rolling around in it, get up
and breathe, just practising this will fill your life up steadily for months, while later on
getting distracted is better—as on a long drive to the seaside when after tedious hours
the upside-down triangle of navy blue is glimpsed, jammed hard into the V of the land
and a glad cry goes up, the car-sick infant groans but she still gets reluctantly interested
despite herself, and longs for sand and fish and chips and roundabouts again—
next become mildly malicious in studying the failed consolations of middle age
that at least some of the people you once mistakenly went to bed with and *v.v.*
now sometimes look seedier, more despairing than you, though that's only
because you get to use lipstick and hair-dye whereas they on the whole do not—
your vanities, and pleasure in theatrical self-blame, have got you where you are today
that's here: and though you've noticed now that you can breathe again, you do

vi FLIP, FLOP

What clicks and rattles coloured strings of plastic curtains all the afternoon.
What writes down 'vanish' and then worries that 'varnish' might have been
more truthful or at least prettier—from where I sit, exactly what's the difference
                                        between the two? I have to know.
What is it that I inch down, like a mouse under the tranquil throat of a snake.
—Be quiet it's a kind of work isn't it, so work, eat flies, and love your children.
Although they too will leave you they're always leaving you, you guano monument.

vii Disintegrate me

There was such brilliance lifting off the sea, its aquamarine strip
blocked in behind white-dashed mimosas, that it stung my eyes
all morning as I stood in the old playground, pushing the swing
steadily, looking out across the water and longing to do without
these radio voices, and without my post as zealous secretary, as
transmitter of messages from the dead, who'd issue disclaimers
that they'd ever sent them—all the while a slow hot cut spreads
to baste me now with questions of my own complicity in harm
muttering thoughtfully about 'patterns' until I'm stamped out as
an old paisley shawl or worn kelim, do I look good as this one
or should I be less loud, or less repetitive? and on the top of my
wardrobe, familiar spirits cluster and hang to chatter, lean over
to peer down interestedly at me, vivaciously complaining about
the large amounts of fluff I've left up there, 'that's just as we'd
expect': meanwhile the out-to-kill person is not, or so she or he
shrugs, pulled at by voices, but dead at heart stands amnesiac
plumped out with the effective innocence of the untroubled—
This gloss is taking me on unconvincing dashes down blind
alleys I mistrust, since desperate to see things straight, I can't fit
apt blame in to self-damnation: could I believe instead in drained
abandon, in mild drift out over some creamy acre studded with
brick reds, to be lifted, eased above great sienna fields and born
onward to be an opened stem or a standing hollow, a flesh ring
through which all slips or a fluent cylinder washed through by
azure-tangled braid, trailing Stella Maris, fervent star of the sea
marine milk vessel flopped at the lip flicking down swathes of
gulls emulsifying blackened earth striped and coiled under rock

under burnt straw air fuzzed in breathy fields of coconut-sharp
gorse flowers flushed tan on cliffs where lower toothpaste green
lucidly rears and rears to the crash of blinding crumpled water
smoothing to clear and flat; so calmly let me disperse so simply
let me disperse drawn out thin-frothed in a broad lacy pancake
fan of salt, or let me fall back as dolphins rock back in the sea
twirled like slow toys on pin-wheels—No single word of this
is any more than decoration of an old self-magnifying wish
to throw the self away so violently and widely that interrogation
has to pause since its chief suspect's sloped off to be cloud, to be
wavery colour bands: no 'release from service to a hard master'
said of the thankful close, it's hoped, of sexual need in oldest age
can touch this other drive of shame fighting to clear a name to itself:
it can't, because its motor runs on a conviction that if I understood
my own extent of blame then that would prove me agent: it doesn't
want to face a likely truth of helplessness—that the inflated will to
gauge and skewer each wrong turn may blank out what's far worse
to bear: impersonal hazard, the humiliating lack of much control—
I don't get past this thought with any confidence.

John Riley

at the Stanley Spencer exhibition

the plants succulent , distinct , each in its own atmosphere
announcing planthood in a tended garden
with blossoming trees a variation on the theme
or fields again ripe with harvest
what language — or harvest — allows you to express
and then begin : start with fools , a likely start ,
wounded as chrysanthemums , caught in our own shadows
though there are windows could open
and hands grow delicate in opening
the worst wound is love   clouds , cloud over
as a journey returned from   or started

travel notes

impossible to be silent , impossible to speak
ritual of light holds memory of darkness
in itself and we , we cling to darkness
that chestnut sapling about to burst into leaf
has more truth than I ; burst of flame
to be followed by green , flame reaching
outwards and upwards , an offering of itself
road unrolled like a wet ribbon through the fields
and a heron , always the same one
fishes motionlessly in this rain
that spreads the light evenly   now are
all things made

river full and brown
concept , sound and invocation
coincide in word , in dusty blackthorn

some things so simple : these are the paths I walk on every day
there's where the dog chases squirrels

my wife breathes under the same roof
interpretations flicker about them : got you!
no , never , never simple enough for that but when the wind
                                        drops suddenly
now it's booming through the trees , now it's quite gone
there in that space is what I take to be a laughter
as the dome of Hagia Sophia ,
stone letting light through

the dog moves in his sleep , settling the day's accounts
above this square flat roof the sky
peels off layer after layer of time
vertigo no less and here am I
unable to settle
making a bad job of expressing joy

summer seeming

everything can be grown from seed—only stipulation
is if the seed's diseased . this greasy turf , no
bowlers' footholds , how the childless also figure
in the generation game , dark warm words rise
from the mid-day soil cut across by a cool breeze , gratefully
gulp them down . summer seeming , endless
search for a rhythmic foothold , a familiar gratefully
accepted . provided . ask no questions . answer no questions .

now what a dawn unfurls , every surface
wet , glistening . the armchair just holds my body
though it could seat someone bigger .
the essential oil of the plants or herbs employed :
a couple of pieces a day . a day ! drip , drip ,
two by two , two by one , a cloud-growling ,
a green automatic and finally
no play at all today .

for the rain , you see , a notation dotted
across every chair in the landscape
and perfectly neutral what the bloody hell
to do with emotions . birds dive about—dive
into a respectable dive , drink given

words gratefully , could be worse , a breathing space ,
smugness of fair seed-time pounds ,
it pounds and is not satisfied .

the sky temporary though it may be
fills in well , benches lurid , wasps wait
people retire to cars trees in vee
formation keep static perspective
as why not , flower-beds , crisp bags it goes on
image born in as insistently as sheet rain :
acceptance not enough , inheritance , continuation
why move , why not move , wind tears through upper branches
each atmosphere cloyed how can you tell
one skin from another . wind grows in violence

once
success is beauty

autumn sunshine , clawed hand on the morning paper
traces explosions of desire , the human
lineaments : she killed herself , dreaming
of her Tunisian lover   the Canon
attacked for standing aside , with God ,
from the world

we were what you are —
you will be what we are

a bread strike a power strike — then sun strike rain
strike angels' strike ? eternity , that is , today ,
comes out to meet us with such aids

dog's skull dreams softly , guarded by paws
dreams in no time at all

unstoppable splendour waves
work in one after another and earth
makes ready to sail

after sky

that is , today

Peter Riley

Elf Shots

Now the table is set, a covenant to endure
just by heartening now and wish to be
devoutly even, much as my face hurts
today; it has all been bought with means.
Now the table's laid I can't leave it,
tea towel over my shoulder like a loose
bra strap, guardian of this vale where
we try not to be eaten by the food, not
too much. The divinity of that certainly
isn't prudential, in fact the whole band
knows itself by its vast appetite and
how openly it closes; local time
or motherlove brought to conclusions
sealed under the inverted teacups to
make possible what is lived: a new love
not transferred from anywhere, peculiar in
every facet to us, and is itself that which
concludes the forgone mysteries, complete
or not, this thick new life is the lid.
Oh clamp it constantly at the forge of
constancy, otherwise this holy day is
pure bank, our very care of the child trans-
gressed into fear for the deposit. For even when
the hedges darken and speedwell and concrete
glow in dim patches still is the traveller
attended, through magnetic garden and
retail glade a human spark struck off
the fossils themselves darts over and back
tracing the head arch, wild over
hymen's shore my God behind me entirely
to come, the moon after all. This cuts
the oil routes. Informations and
the layers of residue, so much resented, break
at veins and bridges across which
your heart is plainly mine, just

a little pecked en route. Very lust,
cloaked in tar, is our frontier man
and the wish its own sufficient caution
as messenger from the sky cists wanting us
home. Pavilions and abattoirs beam with
gain below the town and rail trucks
clank in the night—who would claim the least
victory or aught redemption from the state we
all inhabit like something fallen from a lorry?
Victims, losers, we come back talking of
truth meaning only that you and I love this
earth we die of, the human garden set aslant
the starry gradients, the scarred night.
Trim the border as you reach it to the ghosts
of outside, usufruct; guard that and the house
is ready. The kettle steams forth, light on
the far hill concertinas, the butter holds
its breath, the bread stretches to Hell.
Yes, we shall be even. Sit down and fall to

from *Alstonefield V*

Another damp Sunday morning up and walk over
Pea Low (another distressed tumulus) and what's
that flicker in the distance? what's that
clump of reflection west of the village? Why
were the roads so busy this morning it was
England Now: petrol flicks the work-day whip
and we poor peasants dive for the verge.
Cut short the walk, curve under Gratton Hill
and return, for the battle's up—it's that
trough in time, it's a Car Boot Sale!

It is difficult to know the good in lives.
If I'd found a rare glass I might have gone
chirruping to Stoke and the dour Sweeny. That
remains unproven. Dull English weather,
the day stands inert, colour stops dead,
distance diffused, a green field and a shed
with the usual water tank at the back of a farm
in the mud. It would be specious to pretend

that any bit of British countryside is anything
but an agricultural factory marked Piss Off.

And people open their car boots to reveal
image destitution. But a true ring, a
soul lock, and shopping is a delight, what
traces left of tribal pain lessen in the rain
until every necessary transaction brandishes
the rose of time, triumphantly above
the stalls of love. Then the heart and the
mountain ring are one. What if the inter-
vening nonsense turned out to be a small
entertainment called City of Fear?

Intervening nonsense called western culture
longing to die rather than face the world-
opening it initiated. Dampening I turn down
a plastic shepherdess at 30p and go back
to the car. And sit waiting in the rain
for something better than metonymy, some-
thing less fairground and more circus,
something to take the truth of the west-
ern world out of its pocket and purchase
life everlasting or a well meant Friday hug.

No use waiting, turn the key, go. Where?
If I went North I'd live in a cold music
for guitar and steel-works and have to face
daily a narrower question over the silver moors,
the treasure chests of bird and slow thought
where the houses cling to the long ridges
trying to teach Coleridge that sublimity
isn't vertical after all, but carries grey
rock-juice down into heavenly furrows where
bright minerals sing for dinner, home and away.

Or to speak plainly, pennies are good shit.
If I went West you wouldn't notice me, a
Sunday fisher in the canal, a packed-lunch
gourmet who goes back to a brick row with
small back window onto flagged yard and
coke-shed, there to pass the dark hours
in seasonal remembrance. It is a dream

of such fragile substance such unlaundered
currency I daren't speak, the Sweeny man
at the mirror, coated in disinfectant blood.

Then work is the only credit and it's true but if
I go East the whole scale of action is enhanced,
the great keep rises over the plains, on its surface
reptilian armature twined formally with affection
shield against shield, eye and ear stretched to
soul-pitch across the sky, and all the trim fields
dissolve into the slow riches of decay. The fewness,
the shifting drone of death, lines a shared crown
on an innocent forehead — patient scholar, mongol
child, and working ploughman, designate the world.

I couldn't go there today, the theatre is hidden
under Restoration scaffolds. I could go South,
to the heart of smooth success, and deny the grit
of presence, evade the friction of self-surface
against a viable universe, don't take me there.
Please don't deliver me to that small south, that
smilybox where language oils itself constantly
to idio-defeat; let me wander still in the open
fields of failure, where the linnet coughs at eve
and the daffydil hides its condom, let me live

Longer in the long pain. I won't go south, I won't
enter the gloss. But I did, I went south, why,
for a library, for fear of provinciality, as if
that meant a thing in the corrosive fog of self
-colonization, because I needed company.
And come back up here three times a year
for humanity. I'll stay where I am, I'll book
myself back to the bee-hunting bee, I'll count
up to fifty and take a deep dinner, followed
by the wine of solitude in the clamoring vale.

È Questa Vita Un Lampo

Wrap the light in tendrons and no one
can take it except finally. So the world
is darkened.

Daily darkened. O blessed man,
that the self flees into
a cave at your anger and the worms

The beneficial worms bite the white rock
to a soil, that holds and sets the stem
of a marriage cup, future cost of

Written flesh—worth every drop
for it opens and tints at the
start of death to the temperature

Of the globe and bears its illustration
from cell to cell unwrapped, casting
back from the body's lack a glow,

Small in grain that blasts fantasy inside
out. And the fuse of this demonstration:
a single pronoun on the doorstep begging no

More than sustenance. Claiming no rights.
Starting no fights. Elegant in red
fur and blue tights.

Maurice Scully

Variations

Once upon a time there were three
billion bears. Ling. Dab.
Who studies happiness

now—busy crazy—who? The ABC
of Letting Go lets go—oh
look—or

deaf to the what-in-what—stunned/
back from the hospital
on the way back too

back to the wall
my old dead
father

summer to winter to
beginning-spring
cutcutcut.

A fist tightened of a
sudden forgetting
itself

opens—glint in the windowpane—
morning—cloudless—
sunlight—

a gull on a chimneypot—
dog in the
garden . . .

but to spend the time just so
dust in the
laneway

shadows across
birdsong
(bus

en route) falling floating-
falling
their

mesh diagonal over
surfaces that
tilt black

ribbons into dark green pools then
wait—answer—expand the
view: Tuesday/sharp.

What you need here are millions of precise steel tools.
[p 255]

At the Question-Wall though at the heart of
the Lattice/Oh let me be
faithful to

your humble among your
polysnobberies
(otherweb

elsewhere take
over take
cover)

—translate then scuff
the slate &
play—

busy crazy too & so my heart
in the constricted thing
(stung) o saisons o chateaux

the petty business of freedom
the solo the
hopeless

& no end to the wriggle of the mind &
no relief whatever anywhere ever
to be had.

So. Born to be slaves & monkeys forever?

I'll go down among the people on foot
tonight/bees in the plum blossoms
busy crazy/

gag the pack-of-dogs thinking
in my head trapped &
travelling in

isolation here/to get to the
temple hot with its punctual
flock   (cut granite)

to get to the company of those never
practising freedom never
or isolation

pen creel hive
fire ice or
to yes

you me everybody
each *isola*
SPACE

I parted my hands to refocus
took pen from jacket
& began to

write down the noises
I thought I could
hear a leaf

make falling hitting
the other
branches

angl-
ed twist-
ing

in the canopy in
transit to land
on my page-

top here on the table-top
bid bead bed bod then/
then delete that oh

just another born-again
quietist waiting to
bite back. But

no. Check the micro-
scope. What? Iris
& lilac.

Wait a minute I only want
six sections with a break at
five & the insertion of this
here would make a seventh in
total &/rest happiness peace/

You me everybody
each *isola*
aching

waking up to/in
desolation in
the grey

nothing of nothing
(touch me) noting
& (dot)

doting over the tight co-woven
anti-original
half-

thing/iris & lilac
busy & crazy. Who studies
happiness now?

Split. So.
Decided.
Together

dotdot wrapped up in
themselves &
about to/

happiness? Back to
the wall. I'll
go down

tonight shedding shredding
the personal
rubbish

that
clung
so

O now I wouldn't do that.

Tiny
temple-silhouette —
crisp serrations —

barely visible. If you look up
do you see heaven?
Once

upon a time. Cling to the
rung. Don't look
down

(to how many teddybears
having how much fun
anyway?)

tree-shimmer tree-towering tree-whisper
tree-cold that shapes &
holds—don't—

in the/it's a destroying fire a supralucent
liquid there if either then
but definitely

four children two adults under a plane tree
in the rain suddenly—
mine—bare—

network of billions of microscopic
delicate precise
dots

in the dance
improvised
& manic

that fits the magnetic lock's
secret internal
crease &

is sucked
into
its

slit/quick/the key
& dissolved
in a hiss

of acidic steam—the sky/sparrows
busy in the clematis on the
wall/

who studies
happiness
now

the needle tickles the vacancy
plum blossoms bees
busy & crazy

sprinkle water/mutter-murmur for solace
happiness where was I? stunned
back o yes

to wet fingers/dance/before entering
& leave before the end of
ceremonies.

                    *

            To
          honour
        the light
        on the
        pool the
        rain made
        on the foot-
        path without
        a sound
        last night
        hardly a
        sound a
        lightness
        outside the
        window out
        of the blue
        flower the
        mind is
        (too) then
        /what must
         we do?/
        then *yes*
        a b c
        touch taste
        this is
        the lifespan
        spread on
        a windowpane
        glisten-spirit
        back &
        forth back
        & forth
        across the

fields to
the hospital
under the
trees whose
pods underfoot
brittle in
the grass
as you
tackle the
echoing/the
hard-nosed
hard-eyed
hard-necked
hard-hearted/
dead-dead
it said
the Crow
loud into
the incinerator/
hang up
Sanity evap-
orate Death/
touched.
Touched
suddenly
suddenly
awake.

*

John Seed

'This Curious Involvement, A Dominant Species'

In memory of John Riley

Smoke twisting over the scorched ground
In the shadow of sky little disc
Ablaze

        through the fields and the hills
Last leaves like snow
                blown through space

Everything converged to this

              silence

       endless play of reflection

Actual tree-root twisting through dry earth

Absolute presence   dazzling, impenetrable

Always there always different in
Human matrix

Little world these quiet woodlands

In a tangle of connections

Happy unhappy coincidence
Eye of the storm

            December 1978

During War, The Timeless Air

the sea shone
and we walked in danger
To the cliff-edge

Soft grass   immensity of cloudless
Space

gulls guillemots   a dark bird
Whose name we never knew

Everywhere
their sound among the white rocks . . .

But we are dumb

Powerless   now totally exposed . . .

Shivering naked into space the

Solitary mind flickers among elements

In silence

For a moment almost free

At the nation's edge
Bede's image of
Was it? a sparrow
Swooping through the bright hall

England May 1982

'From Escomb, County Durham': July 1990

Reporting to a future difficult
To believe exists exactly
Midnight and actual rain

Out there beginning
Somewhere
Saxon car bodies rusting in
Empty yards nettles
Bramble wild roses hawthorn
Along the abandoned railway other
Names probably and blurred
Stonework the medium
Vertical of meaning
Lights the instant
Glitters if what you see
Circular in the organized
Silence diamond
Broaching and chancel arch
Serpent dial

Breathing in   the summer rushing
Past outside

'Best wishes'

Sofia

Someone's absence you
Dreamed cold into airfields a referent
Perlovska cyrillic moonlit key
Jammed twice in the lock in the dark
Chimney stairs shoulders ache colder
And colder
Rust so everything is
Pointless again the next
Flight

2 xi 1993

      shadow of the gable-end
Sharp against the white wall
Fading and shifting
As clouds cross how beautiful
The world seems its transformations
Incomplete as we
Begin to leave

Gavin Selerie

from *Roxy*

23

The angel of moment is dust
between the pages of the text,
rising from rilles and walled plains,
her blue wings poised in ecstatic thrust,
a messenger whose promise is cross-sexed,
mutely trumpeting torch-refrains.

Things and words, not things—
a bra attached to the cockpit
loads the flight with night-talk,
subterranean lips and ears
with an echo of tinkling glass.

Share an acknowledged icon
to bring you through—
brief, filmy, flexible.

Feel, smell what is rechannelled.
The urge to get back is an urge to get on,
you could say it's the V of desire
or simply a wipeout with high decorum.

For these are doors into a circular corridor,
the years brought back with a slight twist,
a suspicion of rot beneath the veneer.

If you came out of prison after fifteen years
you'd see it as freer, faster and more beautiful,
but encyclopedias and double-glazing
might shrink your optics and punish you in silk.

Cut it off, reshape it,

I didn't know whether they were joking:
to push down one dream to release another,
a slave language strained and contorted,
a lottery in which one gets to be
in riding breeches, padded shoulders and jackboots
while the rest are reliably throwaway
like props on a supermarket shelf.
The audit of war has pressed home
the price of everything that breathes.

47

Out of the waste you can spin
a garment of memory, coarser
than an episode in chiffon. It'll reach
between moods, pliant with a grammar
that's never complete. Now enfolds
then—a blip of smalltalk rendering
whole arabias of enchantment, with golden air
in drooping grey. Carry the flamingo
in spear-grass and tongues of acacia,
by a crooked vein over scorched plains.
Venture a life, awake to the gathered yarn,
out-fitting numbers. You go as the spiral
of storks above. Slaggy waves, chance pools,
forests of reeds and ferns, balsam-scented
silence, a crescent of scaly crags
snowcapped. The find is in the dream
by side-steps, fever and a little wild honey:
hail melting at noon. You have it as a child
in the book, if it's not burnt. Mist
over purple pinnacles. Set so
one word brings on another
like dancers hand in hand.

52

Hungry bower of drolleries—
bonework the lie to all—
street-sharp, invention
and wanting more.

Counterfeit, composed, affected,
outside the Big Agenda.
A pair of shoes, a chart song.
An expression not an opinion.
Designer myriads pranked up
speaking in the carriage of their bodies
(dumb shows and prognostics).
Not about necessity but choice:
colours of heavens, stars, planets.
Potent enticers
want to step out.

We are tiffanies, ruff-bands,
coronets, amulets, knots and swimming figures,
juggling strength of metals, stones, odours—
the flash puissant, the lingering cinnamon bark.

Go for sweet surfaces of added value,
take it to the limit
and quit before it peaks.

Robert Sheppard

from *Empty Diaries/Twentieth Century Blues 24*

Empty Diary 1905

She falls for him, conventional longing well
tutored, no pose held, broken but breathing,
yet she keeps a finger in a
page of last year's tightly scribbled diary:
the ranked delights of the Paris corsetière,
the dummies' impersonal whorish display of lace
and china flesh, a flat-buttoned pressing
of chamber-maids' etiquette; can't bear his:
"I sleep, I wake, I never dream"
; wants to slit his throat, to hoist
him, dripping from his penis; her story
stalled, veins in her bare neck pleading.

Empty Diary 1936
The Proletarian News

for Charles Madge

vauxhall was grey she needed blocks of
flats not jewel panopticans she threw back
her hem and did a tight city
fling tyrannical wireless valves on tulip faces

echoes of men patronising answers on folded
blankets heads bubbling with pints of stout
rotten teeth of her voices skin always
gleaming an unblemished marching announcing sore lips

surrealist commodes adorn the scattered floors of
chaotic meal times in houses of the

poor dash of belisha peril in jitters
waiting for the paraffin fire to blow

Empty Diary 1944

Bees at my hive anticipate her hands
defenceless sex the photograph steps back gagged
as Germany confesses dry the voice the
testimony the microphonic guilt sounds so good

Full of arm wrestling girls tough men
tapping you on the shoulder quivering to
Pearl's glitter lashes agitate the hypnotist the
31 metre band you jump jittering jewels

Sky-eyed cyclists creeping parachute beetles stone
faced frozen the sky scars blister Cologne
sequin peaks coloured men dancing off poverty
the Empire those steps sweeping silvery floors

Empty Diary 1954

We are statues of ourselves, stiffened eulogies
in the arthritic history of imperial endeavour
(the world of his syllabics: the words
we silently mouth: our faces networks of

electric lies: our lips would seal: our
eyes close on a world which will
drill its electrodes into our mermaid flesh
sketched in by the boss) Say it:

We lick the pellicle of your absence,
Nazi leather stitching your bulging zip (*stilyagi*
skinny kids shivering outside the wimbledon palais
filter sin through newsprint skin us alive

Empty Diary 1968

"For the man who
        has me . . ."
her eloquent slips black
        my discourse,
this second skin, or
        so she's
been told by her
        second mind.
My tattoo sweats her
        name. She
enters me on a
        useless giggle,
then squats at the
        master controls,
punching slogans into consciousnesses
        sweetened for
rotting the fangs of
        Capital. I
wrote her onto the
        pillow, a
hot boy pressing for
        a kiss,
his Anti-Universe, sunrise from
        her bathrobe;
Or: truncheoned jeers, diesel
        coughs, she's
manhandled into the gaping
        Black Maria.

Empty Diary 1987

        i.m. F.G.

Empowered image Baudrillard
framed by one
new Duchamp urinal
per second dolly-
oracular heroes hammering
MASS-MEDIATING CHAOSMOS

she's "voice" trickling
her absence subverting
the flow of
dominant redundancies paste
book sticky life
worlds vending mermaid
flesh art-thick
fresh referents sing
for lyric shifts
in subjectivity spilling
sky (the hour
glass gravity of
articulate slaves: *she*'s
beautiful on the
executive bed, existential
territory. He's cut
to the balls
at the kitchen
sink, subjective autonomist,
fucks alone within
you, tasteless sucker
of silicone flesh

Empty Diary 1990

Past empty rooms full of men, the
street's alsatian ears pricking up, she searches
for evidence of kindness, but finds annotations
blowing her apart into whatever use her
senses and limbs can make of them.
The smiling professions ease her into loss,
with embalmers' soft assurances, each migratory text
striving to be total. Her lips, pursed,
mouth a public language to parade in.
An alien resident of delirium, adrift in
dialogue, the arguments small but binding, she
lives in voices that aren't hers: *Anything
else*? (Capital's plea.) Pit bulls sniff their
masters' tattoos, as rusted muscles melt in
percussive light. She recalls late capitalism, its
vascular delights. Dogs bark liminal threats to

its exchanges; bland ugliness, it's never enough.
Her voice, stuck in the ventriloquist's gullet,
uses what she finds, takes what she
can use: "There're too many eyes here,
running on empty, too many faces whipping
posts of prohibition. These people too easily
file somebody else's history, their own shadows
jumping out across windscreens to greet them

Colin Simms

The First English Wildcat

July 1972, Northumberland

Wild-cat come-upon
explosive to fill space with stripes and eyes
                    like polished cartridge-brass-end-caps
sunlight
                    through all the little sticks of the old bracken
three suns on one hill.

                    And I woke you from your stillness
both of us afraid, and you stretched away out.

After you had gone, I lay and looked
and saw the trees as fircones, squirrel-stripped,
shed scales, stacked stillness because the birds
scared, had scorched the air when you were near.

                    I fear, for the seed in them:
the eyes, the stripes, the pines, the birds . . .

                    Wild-cat come-upon
coming back into England, brash the corkscrew
of complacent living without such splitting, slit eyes
spit your smile and split our sheaths for miles.

Pallid Harrier

(Rudland Rigg Oct. 1976, for R.H.C.)

Pipits sit up, sprinkle, dont give it motion, stay.
Though they are line men, they are intestate
how they measure space is repetitive
          one slender bird of prey comes on apace

Here less/as on the High Plains/light is level
the underside near as dead as a gullflank grey
though it pulses after prey in hate
and sinews stand out distinct.
Here the way the wind rips bevelled by feather-hand
tip the balance of credulity: beauty can't slay
cant violence is not extinct.
Inevitable as over this tableland
the upturned ironstone weathers cut to gray
though its water runs Red Chalybeate
sand-blawits stand in instinct
show and call after only; stony, bland.

sand-blawits: dialect name for grouse
R.H.C.: Ronald Clark, wind-engineer

from *Shots at Otters*

lochside silverschistsand disturbed-to-black-below distributed
pattern-padded pewter-grade velvet-hollows grains added otter pattern
wind off water levelling sibilant bevelling gritscreen bankscree
whistle   reminding you   of wigeon whee-oo
lifting, see prints between bents-tail-race-slice-silt sift sting
still tracks slow upslope shorten portage not forage but for ages
we newcomers can begin to see pattern   even from this little elevation
braids loosen elements-stream raise islands   bruised-
petal-heartsease-violet trail wakes prospect of please not violence
increasing-in-confidence   bolder heavier just before lost in boulders

    when we were least aware the stiff log dogging windshore
sure-of-his-lie breaks cover sure-of-his-line leans lie of the land over
from under where-couldnot-have-hidden-him right-under-feet wonder
instead left-right losing-using his whole enters not-in-the-line-of-his-head
twisting quick long into the river's plaited-in on-itself longitudinal as time
otters were here before

Loch Maree 1970

Grey Wagtail on the Tyne

the dirtiest, downstream of Team
                                   twinned-for-power   flourmill   turret
Flash lever-long tail lined by the Yellow of it flirt opening-flower or of
                                        butterfly-forewings somewhere else
                                        in sour-air shadow oilcracker tower
Flash of felsite arching shine of the Grey and White not at some torrent's tumbling fellside
                                     not at a milecastle of the Roman Wall's marchings.
Not where you would expect it, mountain light and air or brightening some rock gloom
but here   shadowstabbing to show the broom and gorse
                                     starting to spurt here out of the dirt
(under the High Level arches the year's first Yarrow already there)
                                         and of course
we reject 'message'   out of the coarse comes forth the fine
to accept presage   to the new beauty comes the new line

                                         (with Dana, May 77)

COLIN SIMMS   245

Iain Sinclair

from *The Ebbing of Kraft*

ocean estate

fording pondlife to pamper your Arab steed
rosettes displayed above pillows
of cleanest straw—can't call
a whippet a dog (it's a bitch anyway &
hot enough to smear my shiny strides)
call it: 'longterm rewards of academic life'

all the blood fruit wine that
flatters & does not grind the loaf you
squeeze cutting a pinbone pet
who has mislaid her bell

"forest" is no threat so much green
stacked until you close out
the other stuff the bearded
litigant poets incubating harm (despoiling
place) too pedigree'd to fart in tune

poets outgun symposium novelists
having less to say & saying it
with more conviction & smelling
like they *live* by choice in mismatched
suits (obligated to Burton's black)

the fust of old books & older cheese
nobody loves gossip like these salaried dudes

above us hangs a carmine cloud
the amputated leg of Harry Crews
stern invoice of what a writer's career
should entail—no kids & a drawful of
biro caps to clean the wax from your ears

granted, all dream
but some of you, having better manners,
would never admit so much

14.V.95.

snow lip

for forgery, once, in Rutlandshire
—ANGELA CARTER

bird-creole or the billowing froth of bride song
privately parsed & since unheard
from antechamber & dubious balcony caught
in bloody dew by the sheet-examiners, rare
music to the sweaty hair-man who excuses himself
to boast piss & dip his scalded organ
in the athanor's cruel furnace

overlook a vitreous pier beyond which
the sea is hard as remembered fire
curvature like the arm of an handless groom who
reaches across the alabaster pillow & cries
"touch me for our saviour's sake," kicks against
the lion stool that anchors his fretful sole

willing or not, the lake is artificial (as is her eye)
patterns of random magnetism
deform the church tower shattered by chopper blades
a showy landing in the wrong field:
mortal diners lay aside their forks, await measurement
white suits & parasols, not grasping what *that* portends

housewives juggle table plates
disguise penile shavings of pink fish-fruit
bile grapes & meat-ripe droppings,
take silver spoon & scoop the dripping clag of ash
into the infanta's generous bodice, manhandle fur

"nothing phases the river" he moans
drowning in his liar's blackened teeth

6.ii.96

IAIN SINCLAIR   247

world's oldest comedian is dead

Barbers are murdered in the night!
— GREGORY CORSO

walking through wet wheat an ocean of mercury after
the storm's head had snapped in the wound a
blunt spike driven deep into brain jelly — geography
of desire, sperm-tails photographed as galactic reductions
fetishes & footsore hyphens, delightful shoes,
neck-braces & mandrakes preserved in smoky bottles
disengage, alchemy & the alchemist, red sand — Russian
in name only, sour silk drenched under coarse
serge, Comrade Commissar, "give us a twirl"
vile officer-class peons with cowshit on their boots
perform in flawless French while swilling
wineglasses whole, best red, *fin* on the broad screen
a word not a bite, a signal to pull back that ungloved hand
from its almond-oil trespass, the tongue from the cheek
it spells refreshed light outside the fire door shaken
into coats, rain stalled, horn buttons undone
a loose belt, odd legs negotiating the cobbled slope
beneath an undistinguished church — a shark
in the shallows of a coffee-shop, mirrors everywhere
new underwear discreetly disclosed before it is discovered
(& distressed), another disappointing rhubarb *brûlée*
as preamble to permitted violation, the ghost of a girl
in the doorway of a small hotel, thanking us
for not contributing to her relief, the cocky Irishman
scoring a quid, hard coin, at the traffic lights
heraldic spoon twirling the coffee rust to glacial sand
"my ignorance has been well preserved"

9.iii.96

a serious of photographs

in the 'first book-length study of the work' of jh prynne
the name of simon armitage appears as
(in)frequently as that of paul celan. discuss

I don't for example consider that poets are
rock 'n' roll old or new he
said apologetically quite the reverse
(another case altogether to drop from the carousel)
duty declared & all charms to ward off
the fear of flying fit in a nicely printed
carrier bag (later a head-caul or sex aid) (later still
a surveillance shield against nuclear sunburn)
& can you tell me, the unident grinned
the nature of your business at the fibre optic
satellite of Gravesend — not yet not ever
the elevated cage transcends a chalk bowl
the sepulchral stone of dr field steps up
the side of the church tower (needlessly barred)

Kent 'rolling' away. England he gasped
let's come back with a camera as
if we could — no time
for a teabreak in Tel's the rusty
pick-up of the water tower no trout in the pool
just a wren-brown barmaid's unshifting breast
all that artifice adds to nature
geezers in white t-shirts & gold chains
holding corn the scarlet poppies the hymn of pylons
tide surges around a fixed post & the noise
of the dead is everywhere overwhelmingly absent

13.vii.96

Chris Torrance

Acrospirical Meanderings in a Tongue of the Time

The tyranny of fuel. Up & down, round & round, merrygoround,
marigold. What is my own mind? The causal cone's* base weight
presses down on me. A tinkle of lightning
on radio circuits. As clouds red
over a stormy sunset shift. Squirrel twists away round the trunk
under which I find *Boletus luridus & Russula atro purpurea.***
Hare whips from cover in fierce spray as I cross the wet field.
Judgment its own madder yellow. The insatiable fire.

October 1970

*Note on 'The Gyres,' by Richard Ellmann in *The Identity of Yeats*: '. . . A single cone appears as a
principal symbol in Henry More's poem "Psychathanasia," which Yeats must have read; for More
the cone represents the universe, with God at its base & the potentialities of matter at its point:
"Lo! here's the figure of that mighty Cone,
From the Straight Cuspis to the wide-spread Base
Which is even all in comprehension."'
**Boletus luridus & Russula atro purpurea* are varieties of edible wood mushroom.

*

It is difficult to exaggerate the importance of mushrooms as food, for they
contain ergosterol in large quantities—this is the raw material as it were of Vi-
tamin D. Mushrooms also contain large proportions of sulphur & calcium &
they are the nearest approach to meat in the vegetable kingdom.

—MRS. C. F. LEYEL, *Elixirs of Life* (Faber)

"It Is Difficult to Exaggerate the Importance of Mushrooms as Food"

Accelerated leaf fall   October looks like
sweet ripe summer flesh about to blow

& from the old iron & concrete bridge we followed
a little-used track into the forest
which led to a now-dead homestead, the roof gone,
nettles sprouting in tangy confusion amidst the rubble

spore print of mushroom in the retina, in my dreams
lens displacement in the multi-cellular dark
abyssal sound of leaves in the wind
rushing cloud dance before the sky closes in,
opaque as milk, drifting down noiseless rain
"Once again he searched the clear, liquid eyes
of his tormentor
& tried to read there
evidence, *any* evidence of his intentions
as if he could possibly foresee that demon's
next playful whim."
Flowing molten rivers of red gold
& now the sorrowing impulse . . .

October 1970

Gael Turnbull

Residues: Thronging the Heart

thronging the heart

with utter astonishment
for expression

and on the face of a motorcyclist,
brought into Casualty, who'd missed a
turn, hit a lamp-post, his forehead
split down the centre, the eyes
hanging out

indeed, a sight

a form of utterance, an expression

an abrupt clarity

coming home from work, the Hills
against the sun: a blot of indelible
ink, indigo on carmine

down the centre, headlong

today, tomorrow or the day after,
falling abruptly into place

staining the memory
assailing

out of the commonplace, on impact,
unforeseen

indelibly and sometimes
even of trivia

with a gift of dandelions a child
picked and gave for my birthday,
staining my fingers, the marks
persisting

in the crannies lingering,
little streaks of happiness

or of surprise, and in names, in
each particular: a Jog Scray, a
Wallower, a Smutter — all parts
of a water mill

in a drench of words
and those uncommon

filling the corners, crevices,
crannies of what might

with the first reply
to the first question

by the old worthies of the Kirk:
to glorify — that is, sublime,
transform

and in each particular

like Beastie Dovey of Bringsty
who made a cardboard bassoon
and replied to query: not for
the sound but to learn the
fingering

no less, no more

until left out in the rain to
come apart at a breath yet
unforgettable

that is, by force of intent,
an alchemy

with every moment less, one
less from eternity

so may we love, be loved
unreasonably, to distraction

in bewilderment at each touch,
each parting, wrapt round by
absence, clutching

seized by each pulse,
each breath awakening

hearing the alarm, almost not
hearing, to wake to go out to the
cold, to daily toil, leaving her
bed, still dark of winter

who didn't ask to be born

spewed to the light, a fish
thrust on a shore

expiring in the air,
wrapt in a void

where we were borne by chance of
tide, to make our home, who have
none other

stumbling to rest,
not needing further

while doing something else perhaps,
breaking kindling, buying bread,
tying a shoelace even, realizing

thrust of what must

with a great pain flooding over
us at the sight of so much beauty,
that country called Arcadia, where
we'd stumbled

helplessly thronged
to need each other

      with gaps in the haze, in the
      dawnlight glimpsed, one sight

plume of the breakers,
shoreward

      thronging the heart

There are Words

for a particular size of stone about the size of your fist
for water only just enough to cover something
for little walks which an invalid could be expected to take

for a rocky hillocky bit of land still capable of cultivation for the
    most part
for a small triangular piece of land that can be ploughed only on
    one side
for land from which two crops have been taken in succession

for the left hand side of a furrow
for half of a pair
for the night after tomorrow night

which have been recorded in word lists
compiled on the outer islands with spoken examples
from old persons who still had their wits
in a language not even my grandparents understood;

and shall our descendants some day
be curious to know the words we have,
though I have not found them, giving examples
and idiom of use, explaining the context

for the sort of attention needed driving on a motor-way
for the attention driving slowly on a winding country road
for driving to and from work as you have done perhaps too often

for land approved for development but still standing idle
for land that attracts subsidy provided it stands idle
for land that has been re-zoned and is suddenly valuable

for the time you get for the smallest coin
for the simultaneous programme on the other channel
for a duplicate of a duplicate

for delight in remarking on small details
for the enjoyment of exploring dictionaries
for the indulgence of finding words?

Takings

As sea.. rain
earth.. dust
fire.. stubble
silence.. us.

Catherine Walsh

Nearly Nowhere

Well it's half-past
hangin' time/time to
go rob

S'what the old lady sd. to me

Encapsulate it
and escape it

Timeless

Even /reiterate it

Half-past
hangin' time/time to
go rob

from *Pitch Part Three*

matter
of fact
        poetical
                fabulous

            time

    of the mind

        making
over instants

    (   )
    stasis

absorption
(in terms of saturation)
farts in a bath

  realize
this is not memory
conditions
the state of the subject at
the moment
in question   being

making pictures
to walk into wide
edging   on

the village to the bridge the terminus to the
Rialto the bird to the shop the road to
the house this is the same place over
the hill hospital bridge grassed canal topping
drowned children weeds the Big House in place
of kitchen gardens sloped terraces
6 houses to Portmahon

having not forgotten
smell colour
of eye
hair tone
flesh
having not forgotten
there should be
some where eye
hair colour of
voice smell
having not forgotten
some where tone
of eyebrow lash
there should be
colour it should
be clear some
where forgotten
there white shirts
opening flap
having
not forgotten
standing where
some be
left

that's all
it rhymes with

wet roof clear brown beyond
buffeted flowers till light changed
shade tone more than grey effectively
impeding adumbration moving
lines space (racing point to point)
how many in or out does it take
each an anchorage in view of the
wind (the sea) marathon
railway line sea side of a lonely
night walking dark rocks shift water
breaks

half the way
home
on one
way streets

from *A Wait*

old anorak green
leaves bent over
themselves
            now
opening out
pointing left

now rolling in their
sides military grey
      veering right tree
back house side
road cargo line
   town

                    well it's not an important idea
rather
equate
        could this be/burbling
        here

event
creak
bang   feature here more
      facet space

   voices all   well put down   then

put down   wanted
reading
                heeded speed over sidereal time

   as blab on blurb is wont
   this is not time
   place meaning less
   alienation
   area one
   created
   to

   self

is it?
unit
now bringing diverse tendencies
heel
no round tablecrap work
done refined repeated
unit
now bringing mathematically
inappropriate syllogisms
eat

Benjamin Zephaniah

Speak

Yu teach me
Air Pilots language
De language of
American Presidents
A Royal Family
Of a green unpleasant land.
It is
Authorised
Approved
Recycled
At your service.
I speak widda bloody tongue,
Wid Nubian tones
Fe me riddims
Wid built in vibes.
Yu dance.

The SUN

I believe the Blacks are bad
The Left is loony
God is Mad
This government's the best we've had
So I read The SUN.

I believe Britain is great
And other countries imitate
I am friendly with The State,
Daily, I read The SUN.

I am not too keen on foreign ones
But I don't mind some foreign bombs
Jungle bunnies play tom-toms,

But, I read The SUN.

Man, I don't like Russian spies
But we don't have none
I love lies,
I really do love Princess Di
I bet she reads The SUN.

Black people rob
Women should cook
And every poet is a crook,
I am told—so I don't need to look,
It's easy in The SUN.

Every hippie carries nits
And every Englishman love tits
I love Page Three and other bits,
I stare into The SUN.

I like playing bingo games
And witch-hunting to shame a name
But aren't newspapers all the same?
So why not read The SUN.

Don't give me truth, just give me gossip
And skeletons from people's closets,
I wanna be normal
And millions buy it,
I am blinded by The SUN.

Biobibliographies

JOHN AGARD (b. 1949)
Born in Guyana, Agard came to Britain in 1977, and is now widely known as
poet and performer. He won the Casa de las Americas Prize in 1982 and a Paul
Hamlyn Award in 1997. He is currently living in Sussex with his wife Grace
Nichols. His books include *Mangoes and Bullets* (Pluto 1985) and most re-
cently *From the Devil's Pulpit* (Bloodaxe 1997).

TONY BAKER (b. 1954)
Tony Baker was born on J. S. Bach's birthday in 1954, in Merton, South London.
After studying in Cambridge and Durham (where he completed his doctorate
on William Carlos Williams), he has made a living playing the piano in Derby-
shire and the Loire Valley, where he is currently living with his wife and children.
His books include *A Bit Brink Green Quartz-Like* (Pig Press 1983) and *Scrins*
(Pig Press 1989) and an extensive, unpublished prose work on mushrooms.

ANTHONY BARNETT (b. 1941)
Born in London, Barnett has worked abroad for some years as a percussionist in
the field of improvised music. His books include a collected poems *The Rest-
ing Bell* (Allardyce, Barnett 1987) and a collection of poetry and prose *Carp
and Rubato* (Invisible Books 1995). *The Poetry of Anthony Barnett* (ed. Michael
Grant, Allardyce, Barnett 1993) collects essays and other documents with an in-
terview. He edited Veronica Forrest-Thomson's *Collected Poems and Transla-
tions*, and his translations include volumes by Anne-Marie Albiach and Andrea
Zanzotto. He has also published work on the violin in jazz and improvised
music. He is editor for Allardyce, Barnett Publishers.

RICHARD CADDEL (b. 1949)
Born in Bedford and brought up on the Medway Estuary, Kent, Caddel moved
to the northeast of England as a music student in 1968. He currently works as a
librarian in Durham University, where he is also a founding director of the
Basil Bunting Poetry Centre, and director of Pig Press. He has edited Bunting's
Complete Poems (Oxford University Press 1994). His own work includes *Sweet*

Cicely (Taxus 1983), *Uncertain Time* (Galloping Dog 1990), and *Larksong Signal* (Shearsman 1997).

CRIS CHEEK (b. 1955)
Born in London, recently moved to Lowestoft, on the Suffolk Coast. He has worked as a printer, poet, dancer, musician, teacher, and gardener. *The Music of Madagascar* (which he wrote and presented for BBC Radio) won a Sony Gold Award in 1995. Widely known as a performer, his published work includes *First Body of Work* (Bluff Books 1978), *Cloud Eyes* (Microbrigade 1991), and a CD *Skin upon skin* (Sound & Language 1997).

THOMAS A. CLARK (b. 1944)
Born in Greenock, Scotland, Clark has for many years lived with his wife Laurie in Nailsworth, Gloucestershire, where they run Moschatel Press and Cairn Gallery. Books include *A Still Life* (Jargon Society 1977), *Madder Lake* (Coach House Press 1981), and *Tormentil and Bleached Bones* (Polygon 1993). A selection of his work was included in the Paladin anthology *The Tempers of Hazard* (Paladin 1993, with Barry MacSweeney and Chris Torrance).

BOB COBBING (b. 1920)
Born in Enfield, Bob Cobbing has produced a steady stream of visual and verbal poetry since 1942 — all works intended for performance, often with music or dance elements. He is a frequent performer at International Sound Poetry Festivals in Europe and America. His "collected poems" are published in fifteen volumes, each by a different small press in England, Scotland, Wales, Canada, and the United States. Two volumes of selected work are available: *bill jubobe* (Coach House Press 1976) and *bob jubile* (New River Project 1990).

BRIAN COFFEY (1905–1995)
Brian Coffey is now recognised as a leading figure amongst Irish modernist writers. A maths and chemistry graduate of University College Dublin, he gained a doctorate in philosophy, studying with Maritain in Paris. He published his early poetry alongside that of Beckett and Denis Devlin, his contemporaries and friends. Like English and American counterparts such as Bunting and Oppen, he fell silent as a writer after this early career, re-emerging only in the 1960s. A substantial collection of his work, *Poems and Versions*, was published in 1991 by Dedalus Press.

KELVIN CORCORAN (b. 1956)
Kelvin Corcoran is a graduate of Essex University, currently living and teaching in Cheltenham. His work has been much anthologised, and appears in seven collections to date, from *Robin Hood in the Dark Ages* (foreword by Tom Raworth, Permanent Press 1985) by way of *TCL* (afterword by Lee Harwood,

Pig Press 1989) to *Melanie's Book* (afterword by Iain Sinclair, West House/Simple Vice 1996).

ANDREW CROZIER (b. 1943)
Founder of Ferry Press, and editor of formative magazines *The Wivenhoe Park Review* and *The English Intelligencer*, Crozier also co-edited (with Tim Longville) the anthology *A Various Art* (Carcanet 1987). He lives in Lewes, Sussex, and lectures at Sussex University. His books include *Walking on Grass* (Ferry 1969), *Pleats* (Great Works 1975), *High Zero* (Street Editions 1978), and a collected poems *All Where Each Is* (Allardyce, Barnett 1985). A long poem *Free Running Bitch* appeared in *Conductors of Chaos* (ed. Iain Sinclair, Picador 1997).

FRED D'AGUIAR (b. 1960)
Born in London and brought up in Guyana, D'Aguiar trained as a psychiatric nurse before reading English at the University of Kent. He has been Judith E. Wilson Fellow at the University of Cambridge, and Northern Arts Literature Fellow at Newcastle and Durham Universities, and is currently teaching at the University of Miami. As well as poetry, he has written plays and a film, and was a co-editor of *The New British Poetry* (Paladin 1988). His collections include *Mama Dot* (Chatto 1985), *Airy Hall* (Chatto 1989), and *British Subjects* (Bloodaxe 1993).

KEN EDWARDS (b. 1950)
Born in Gibraltar, Edwards has lived in London since 1968, where he earns his living as a freelance journalist. Editor of the magazine *Reality Studios* (1978–1988), he now runs Reality Street Editions with Wendy Mulford. He was a co-editor of *The New British Poetry* (Paladin 1988). He has recently emerged as a composer—several of his recent musical works have been performed by a range of new music groups. His poetry includes *Intensive Care* (Pig Press 1986) and *Good Science* (Roof Books 1992).

PETER FINCH (b. 1947)
Peter Finch was born in Cardiff, where he still lives and practices as poet, short story writer, and bookshop manager. In the sixties and seventies he edited the ground-breaking little magazine *second aeon*. As a performer he has toured with Bob Cobbing and others, and is a member of the performance group Horse's Mouth. He has published over two dozen collections of poetry, including *Selected Poems* (Poetry Wales 1987), *Make* (Galloping Dog 1990), and *Antibodies* (Stride 1998).

ALLEN FISHER (b. 1944)
Active as a poet since 1967, Fisher has also worked as printer and painter (examples of his Fluxus work are in the Tate Gallery collection) and as editor of

Spanner magazine and books. After a considerable period in London (the mainspring of his *Place* sequence 1974–1981), he moved to Hereford, where he teaches at Hereford College of Art. His work includes *Brixton Fractals* (Aloes 1985), *Unpolished Mirrors* (Reality Studios 1986), *Stepping Out* (Pig Press 1989), *Dispossession and Cure* (Reality Street 1994), and *Breadboard* (Spanner 1995).

ROY FISHER (b. 1930)
Fisher was born in Birmingham, which has been an important presence in his poetry since *City* (Migrant Press 1961). His early works (including *The Ship's Orchestra*, 1966, and *The Cut Pages*, 1971) were published by Fulcrum Press; subsequently he was published by OUP (*A Furnace*, 1986; *Poems 1955–1987*, 1988; *Birmingham River*, 1994). A selected poems, *The Dow Low Drop*, appeared from Bloodaxe (1996). Fisher sandwiched a career as a lecturer in American Studies at Keele University between two careers as a jazz pianist. He lives in Derbyshire, and remains, to paraphrase the critic Edward Lucie-Smith, a poet with an international reputation, rather than a national one. He won a Paul Hamlyn Award in 1997.

VERONICA FORREST-THOMSON (1947–1975)
Forrest-Thomson was born in Malaya and grew up in Glasgow. She studied at Liverpool and Cambridge, and taught in Leicester and Birmingham. From 1971 to 1974 she was married to writer and theorist Jonathan Culler. She was killed in a car accident in 1975. Her important critical study *Poetic Artifice: A Theory of Twentieth Century Poetry* was published by Manchester University in 1978. Only one collection of poetry was published in her lifetime: *Language-Games* (1971). Other collections are *On The Periphery* (Street Editions 1976) and *Collected Poems and Translations* (ed. Anthony Barnett, Allardyce, Barnett 1990).

ULLI FREER (b. 1947)
Born in Luneburg, his early work was published under the name of Ulli McCarthy. He currently lives in London, has been a central presence in the Sub-Voicive readings series, and runs microbrigade publications. Recent publications include *Blvd.s* (Equipage 1994) and *eye line* (Spanner 1996).

HARRY GILONIS (b. 1956)
Born and resident in London, Harry Gilonis has written widely on Ian Hamilton Finlay, and is the publisher of Form Books. Publications include *Reliefs* (HardPressed Poetry 1988; reprinted Pig Press 1990), *Pibroch* (Morning Star 1996), *Forty Fungi* (Coracle 1994), and *From far away* (with Tony Baker; forthcoming).

JONATHAN GRIFFIN (1908–1990)

Born in Sussex, Griffin had a career as a journalist and writer on military policy before the war, and as a director of the BBC's European Intelligence during the war. In the postwar period he worked in the British Embassy in Paris. Although his translations (of Camoens, Pessoa, and Char, for example) were respected in the UK, his own work was often best received in the United States, by writers such as Oppen, Rakosi, and Weinberger. His *Collected Poems* was published by the National Poetry Foundation in two volumes in 1989–1990; a selection, *In Earthlight*, was published by Menard Press in 1995.

BILL GRIFFITHS (b. 1948)

Born in Middlesex, Griffiths began composing piano music and poems in the mid 1960s. Encouraged by Eric Mottram and Bob Cobbing he began to publish in the early 1970s, including work such as *War with Windsor* (Pirate Press 1973). Also with Mottram's encouragement he studied English at King's College, specialising in Old English, in which he holds a doctorate. In the early 1990s he moved to Seaham, on the Durham coast—becoming one of the *Future Exiles* (with Allen Fisher and Brian Catling) of the Paladin anthology of that title (1992). His other work includes *Tract Against the Giants* (Coach House 1984) and *Rousseau & the Wicked* (Invisible Books 1996).

ALAN HALSEY (b. 1949)

Born in Croydon, Halsey ran The Poetry Bookshop in Hay-on-Wye 1979–97, a key source for British and American small press material. He runs West House Books, and has published papers on David Jones and Thomas Lovell Beddoes. He now lives in Sheffield. His books include *Perspectives on the Reach* (Galloping Dog 1981), *Auto Dada Cafe* (Five Seasons 1987), *Five Years Out* (Galloping Dog Press 1989), *Reasonable Distance* (Equipage 1992), and *A Robin Hood Book* (West House 1996).

LEE HARWOOD (b. 1939)

Born in Leicester, Harwood grew up in Chertsey, Surrey. His early work flourished in the little magazines of the 1960s, alongside some of his translations of Tristran Tzara, which had been approved by the poet. He has lived at times in Greece and the United States, but since 1967 his home has largely been on the Sussex coast, in Brighton. His publications include *The White Room* (Fulcrum 1968), *The Sinking Colony* (Fulcrum 1970), *Monster Masks* (Pig Press 1985), and *Crossing the Frozen River* (selected poems, Paladin 1988). *Morning Light* is due from Slow Dancer in 1998.

MICHAEL HASLAM (b. 1947)

Born in Bolton, Lancashire, Haslam currently lives in the South Pennines of

West Yorkshire, describing himself as a semi-skilled labourer. He has edited *Open Township* books and magazine. His collection *A Whole Bauble* (Carcanet 1995) includes as its central part the sequence of 84 poems from *Continual Song* (Open Township 1986).

RANDOLPH HEALY (b. 1956)
Healy moved from Scotland to Ireland eighteen months after his birth. He read Mathematics at Trinity College, Dublin, and his first collection *25 poems* was published by Maurice Scully's The Beau Press in 1983. His own imprint, Wild Honey Press, issued his *Rana rana!* and *Arbor Vitae* in 1997.

JOHN JAMES (b. 1939)
Born in Cardiff, James holds degrees from Bristol and Keele Universities, and teaches at Anglia Polytechnic University. Between 1963 and 1969 he edited *R* magazine and books. His own publications include *Striking the Pavilion of Zero* (Ian McKelvie 1975), *Berlin Return* (Grosseteste/Ferry/Delires 1983), and *Schlegel Eats A Bagel* (Equipage 1996).

AMRYL JOHNSON (b. C.1960)
Born in Trinidad, Johnson has lived in England since the age of eleven. She studied at the University of Kent, and has been a frequent performer and writer in schools. A travel book on the Caribbean, *Sequins on a Ragged Hem*, was published by Virago. Poetry includes *Long Road to Nowhere* (Sable 1982; new edition with different work Virago 1985), *Tread Carefully in Paradise* (Cofa 1991), and *Gorgons* (Cofa 1992).

LINTON KWESI JOHNSON (b. 1952)
Born in Jamaica, Johnson came to England in 1961. He read Sociology at Goldsmiths College, London. Coiner of the phrase "dub poetry," he has performed widely with a range of backing bands and musicians. His publications include *Inglan is a Bitch* (Race Today 1980) and *Tings an Times* (Bloodaxe/LKJ Music 1991), as well as a number of recordings.

TOM LEONARD (b. 1944)
Born in Glasgow, Leonard began to write poetry in Glasgow dialect in the late 1960s. His *Radical Renfrew* (1990) is a reconstruction of about sixty West Scotland writers, undertaken whilst writer-in-residence at Renfrew Libraries, and he has also written *Places of the Mind: The Life and Work of James Thomson* (B.V.) (Cape 1993). His collections include *Intimate Voices* (Galloping Dog 1984, republished by Cape 1995) and *Reports from the Present* (Cape 1995). A CD of Leonard reading his own poetry is due for release from AK Press, San Francisco.

TONY LOPEZ (b. 1950)
Lopez grew up in Brixton, South London, at a time when "great games could be played on the bomb sites remaining from the blitz." As a freelance writer in the 1970s he published five crime and science fiction novels with New English Library. He studied at Essex and Cambridge, and is currently Reader in Poetry at the University of Plymouth. Amongst his criticism is *The Poetry of W. S. Graham* (Edinburgh University Press 1989). His poetry includes *A Handbook of British Birds* (Pig Press 1982), *Stress Management* (Boldface Press 1994), and *False Memory* (The Figures 1996). He held a Wingate Scholarship in poetry for 1996/1997.

ROB MACKENZIE (b. 1964)
Born in Glasgow and raised on the Isle of Lewis, MacKenzie is currently doing research in atmospheric chemistry at the University of Cambridge. *The Tune Kilmarnock* appeared in 1995 from Form Books; a larger collection, *Off Ardglas*, is due from Form Books and Invisible Books in 1998.

BARRY MACSWEENEY (b. 1948)
Born in Newcastle upon Tyne, MacSweeney left school at sixteen and worked on the *Newcastle Evening Chronicle*, where he met Basil Bunting. Since then he has worked as investigative journalist and sub-editor on a variety of provincial newspapers. His books include *The Boy from the Green Cabaret Tells of His Mother* (Hutchinson 1968), *Odes* (Trigram 1978), *Blackbird* (Pig Press 1980), *Hellhound Memos* (Many Press 1983), and *Pearl* (Equipage 1995). *The Book of Demons* (Bloodaxe 1997) won him a Paul Hamlyn Award.

BILLY MILLS (b. 1954)
Born in Dublin, Mills spent nine years abroad teaching English as a foreign language in Barcelona and Eastbourne, and is now once more in Eire, in Tallaght, Dublin. With his wife Catherine Walsh he runs hardPressed Poetry, and distributes alternative Irish poetries. His work includes *Letters from Barcelona* (Dedalus 1990), *The Properties of Stone* (Writers Forum 1996), and *Five Easy Pieces* (Shearsman 1997).

GERALDINE MONK (b. 1952)
Born in Blackburn, Lancashire, Monk is widely known as a reader and performance artist and is currently living in Sheffield. With Maggie O'Sullivan she published a manifesto in *City Limits*, concluding that "the most effective chance any woman poet has of dismantling the fallacy of male creative supremacy is simply by writing poetry of a kind which is liberating by the breadth of its range, risk and innovation." Publications include *Long Wake* (Writers Forum/Pirate Press 1979), *Tiger Lilies* (Rivelin Press 1986), *The Sway of Precious*

Demons: Selected Poems (North & South 1992), and *Interregnum* (Creation Press 1995).

ERIC MOTTRAM (1924–1995)

London born, Mottram grew up in Surrey and Blackpool, and served as an officer in the Royal Navy during the war, on a battle cruiser in the North Atlantic, and on a minesweeper in Burma. After the war he gained a double first at Cambridge, and taught at universities in Zurich, Malaya, and Groningen before joining King's College London in 1961. From King's he taught generations of poets and writers, some of whom remembered him in *Alive in Parts of the Century: Eric Mottram at 70* (North & South 1994). He edited *Poetry Review* 1972–1975; co-edited *The New British Poetry* (Paladin 1988); and was the author of numerous critical works including *Blood on the Nash Ambassador* (Hutchinson 1989). His poetry includes *A Book of Herne* (Arrowspire 1981), *Selected Poems* (North & South 1989), and *Estuaries* (Solaris 1991). His work is collected in the Eric Mottram Archive, King's College London, which opened in 1998.

WENDY MULFORD (b. 1941)

Mulford grew up in Wales and lived for some years in Cambridge, where she ran Street Editions; she currently works as a freelance writer, living in Suffolk. She is the author of *This Narrow Place: Sylvia Townsend Warner and Valentine Ackland* (Pandora 1988) and edited *The Virago Book of Love Poetry* (1990). She is co-editor (with Ken Edwards) of Reality Street Editions, and her own work includes *Late Spring Next Year: Poems 1979–1985* (Loxwood Stoneleigh 1987) and *Bay of Naples* (Reality Studios 1992).

GRACE NICHOLS (b. 1950)

Nichols was born in Guyana, where she worked as a journalist before coming to Britain in 1977. She has published children's books and novels as well as poetry, and won the Commonwealth Poetry Prize for *The Fat Black Woman's Poems* (Virago 1984). Her other books include *I is a long memoried Woman* (Caribbean Cultural Institute 1983), *Lazy Thoughts of a Lazy woman* (Virago 1989), and *Sunris* (Virago 1996). A selection of her work appeared in *Penguin Modern Poets Volume 8* (1996) with work by Jackie Kay and Merle Collins.

DOUGLAS OLIVER (b. 1937)

Hampshire born, of Scottish ancestry, Doug Oliver has worked as a journalist, a lecturer, a writer, and, secretarially, in a cancer hospital. He is married to American poet Alice Notley and teaches at the British Institute in Paris. He is the author of two novels and a study of poetic prosody, and eight collections of poetry, including *Kind* (Allardyce, Barnett 1987), *Three Variations on the Theme of Harm* (Paladin 1990), and *Penniless Politics* (Bloodaxe 1994). His work has been included in *Penguin Modern Poets Volume 10* (1996) with Denise Riley and Iain Sinclair.

MAGGIE O'SULLIVAN (b. 1951)
Of southern Irish parents, Maggie O'Sullivan moved from London to Hebden Bridge in the early 1990s. An artist, and editor of Magenta Press, she has performed and been published internationally, and has collaborated with a number of artists, dancers, and musicians. She is the editor of *Out of Everywhere: Linguistically Innovative Poetry by Women in North America and the UK* (Reality Street Editions 1996). Her own work includes *Unofficial Word* (Galloping Dog 1988), *In The House of the Shaman* (Reality Street Editions 1993), and *Palace of Reptiles* (forthcoming, Sun & Moon Press).

TOM PICKARD (b. 1946)
Born in Newcastle upon Tyne, Pickard left school at fourteen. With Connie Pickard he established the Morden Tower poetry readings in 1964. A catalyst in Bunting's return to poetry in the mid 1960s, Pickard's first collection *High On The Walls* (Fulcrum Press 1967) has a preface by Bunting. His prose includes *Guttersnipe* (City Lights 1971), *Jarrow March* (with Joanna Voit, Allison & Busby 1982), and *We Make Ships* (Secker 1989). He is a freelance writer and film-maker, currently living in the high Pennine region around Alston. His most recent collection is *Tiepin Eros: New & Selected Poems* (Bloodaxe 1994).

ELAINE RANDELL (b. 1951)
Londoner by parentage, birth, and upbringing, Randell started *Amazing Grace* magazine in the late 1960s with the encouragement of Anthony Rudolph of Menard Press. She is also editor of Secret Books. Qualified as a social worker and art therapist, she is currently a guardian ad litem working with children. She lives in Kent, surrounded by sheep, geese, cats and dogs, and her family. Her earlier work is collected in *Beyond All Other* (Pig Press 1986); a subsequent volume based on her childcare experience is *Gut Reaction* (North & South 1987).

TOM RAWORTH (b. 1938)
Raworth grew up in South London, leaving school at sixteen "out of boredom" and gravitating towards jazz clubs where he played piano briefly. In 1965 he founded Goliard Press with Barry Hall. When he is not travelling in Europe or America, he lives in Cambridge with his wife Val and grandchild Cato. Amongst his numerous books are *The Big Green Day* (Trigram 1968), *Lion Lion* (Trigram 1970), *Act* (Trigram 1973), *Writing* (The Figures 1982), *Tottering State* (The Figures 1984; revised ed. Paladin 1988), and the bilingual *from Eternal Sections/as Teascain den tSioraiocht* (hardPressed 1990; to mark his Irish passport).

CARLYLE REEDY (b. 1938)
American born, and educated in the United States and France, bilingual
Reedy has been resident in the UK since 1964 and is widely known as a per-
former and multimedia events artist. Her work includes *Sculpted in This World*
(Bluff Books 1979), *The Orange Notebook* (Reality Studios 1984), and *Obituar-
ies and Celebrations* (Words Worth Books 1995).

DENISE RILEY (b. 1948)
Born in Carlisle, Denise Riley lives in London with her three children and
teaches at Goldsmiths College. Her prose books include *War in the Nursery*
(Virago 1983), *"Am I That Name?" Feminism and the Category of "Women" in
History* (Macmillan 1988), and the editing of *Poets on Writing: Britain
1970–1991* (Macmillan 1992). Her poetry collections include *Dry Air* (Virago
1985) and *Mop Mop Georgette* (Reality Street Editions 1993). She is included in
Penguin Modern Poets Volume 10 (1996) with Douglas Oliver and Iain Sinclair.

JOHN RILEY (1937–1978)
Born in Leeds, John Riley began to learn Russian whilst on National Service in
the Royal Air Force from 1956 to 1958. He read English at Pembroke College,
Cambridge from 1958 to 1961, and subsequently became a schoolteacher in or
around Cambridge, and then in Bicester near Oxford. Together with Tim
Longville he ran *Grosseteste Review* and Grosseteste Press, returning to Leeds
at the end of the 1960s. In 1973 he made a brief but important visit to Istanbul,
and in the same year he married. He was received into the Orthodox Church
in 1977. In October 1978 John Riley was killed by muggers near his home in
Leeds. His work includes translations (of Holderlin and Mandelstam) and col-
laborations with Tim Longville, and seven collections of poetry including
What Reason Was (Grosseteste 1970), *Ways of Approaching* (Grosseteste 1973),
and *That Is Today* (Pig Press 1978). His *Collected Works*, edited by Tim
Longville, were published by Grosseteste in 1981; *Selected Poems* (ed. Michael
Grant) appeared from Carcanet in 1995.

PETER RILEY (b. 1940)
Born near Manchester, Peter Riley read English at Cambridge, and has since
lived in Hove, Odense (Denmark), the Peak District, and since 1985 Cam-
bridge, where he runs a bookshop, edits Poetical Histories, and is secretary of
the Cambridge Conference of Contemporary Poetry (CCCP). He has written
studies of Jack Spicer, T. F. Powys, improvised music, poetry, lead mines, and
burial mounds. His poetry has appeared in nineteen collections to date, in-
cluding *Lines on the Liver* (Ferry Press 1981), *Tracks and Mineshafts* (Grosse-
teste Press 1983), and *Alstonefield* (Shearsman/Oasis 1995). A *Selected Poems* is
forthcoming from Salt/Folio.

MAURICE SCULLY (b. 1952)
Born in Dublin, Scully has lived and worked in Eire, Greece, Italy, and Lesotho. He edited *The Beau* magazine, and instigated the Winding Stair readings in Dublin. His work includes *Five Freedoms of Movement* (Galloping Dog 1987), *The Basic Colours* (Pig Press 1994), *Zulu Dynamite* (Form Books 1998), and *Steps* (Reality Street 1998).

JOHN SEED (b. 1950)
Seed grew up in Chester-le-Street, between Durham and Newcastle, out of northeast families. He is currently a lecturer in History at the Roehampton Institute in London, and an editor of the journal *Social History*. His poetry includes *History Labour Night* (Pig Press 1984) and *Interior in the Open Air* (Reality Studios 1993).

GAVIN SELERIE (b. 1949)
Born in London, Selerie is a tutor in the Extra-Mural Department of London University. He has written studies of Charles Olson and Tom McGrath, and edited *The Riverside Interviews*. His poetry includes *Azimuth* (Binacle Press 1994), *Southam Street* (New River Project 1991), and the long sequence (written 1985–1995) *Roxy* (West House Books 1996).

ROBERT SHEPPARD (b. 1955)
Educated at the University of East Anglia, Sheppard now lectures in Writing Studies at Edge Hill University College, Lancashire. He edited *Pages* magazine, and the publication series Ship Of Fools. He co-edited *Floating Capital: New Poets from London* (Potes & Poets 1991). His publications include *The Frightened Summer* (Pig Press 1981), *The Flashlight Sonata* (Stride 1993), and *Empty Diaries* (Stride, 1998).

COLIN SIMMS (b. 1939)
Born in Cleveland, North Yorkshire, Simms attended Keele University. He is a naturalist and writer on motorbikes, publisher of Genera editions, and currently is living in the high Pennines. Published work includes *Pine Marten* (Genera 1973), *Bear Skull* (North York Poetry 1974), *Parfleche* (Galloping Dog Press 1977), *Time over Tyne* (Many Press 1981), *Eyes Own Ideas* (Pig Press 1987), and *Goshawk Lives* (Form Books 1995).

IAIN SINCLAIR (b. 1943)
Born in Cardiff, Sinclair worked as a film-maker briefly before settling in East London as a secondhand book dealer in the late 1960s. He established Albion Village Press, was for a while adviser to Paladin in its poetry series, and edited the anthology *Conductors of Chaos* (Picador 1996). He has published three

novels: *White Chappell, Scarlet Tracings* (1987), *Downriver* (1991), and *Radon Daughters* (1994). His most recent prose work is *Lights Out For The Territory: 9 Excursions into the Secret History of London* (Granta 1997). His poetry includes *Lud Heat* (Albion Village 1975), *Suicide Bridge* (Albion Village 1979), and *Flesh Eggs and Scalp Metal: Selected Poems 1970–1987* (Paladin 1989). His work is included in *Penguin Modern Poets Volume 10* (1996) with that of Douglas Oliver and Denise Riley.

CHRIS TORRANCE (b. 1941)
Christ Torrance was born in Edinburgh and brought up in South London, where he first started to write and be involved in little magazines. In 1970 he moved to the Neath Valley in South Wales, where he has lived since, teaching adult education courses and working with the band Poetheat. His published work includes *Green Orange Purple Red* (Ferry Press 1968), *Acrospirical Meanderings in a Tongue of the Time* (Albion Village Press 1973), *The Rainbringer* (Pig Press 1978), *The Tempers of Hazard* (with Thomas A. Clark and Barry MacSweeney, Paladin 1993), and *Southerly Vector/The Book of Heat* (Cwm Nedd Press 1996).

GAEL TURNBULL (b. 1928)
Born in Edinburgh and raised in northern England and Winnipeg, Turnbull studied Natural Science at Cambridge, and qualified in medicine at the University of Pennsylvania. After a career as a doctor in Northern Ontario, California, London, Worcestershire, and Cumbria, he has retired to Edinburgh. He founded Migrant Press in 1957 and was responsible for much of the interaction between UK and US poetries at that time. His more recent collections include *A Gathering of Poems* (Anvil 1983), *A Winter Journey* (Pig Press 1987), *While Breath Persist* (Porcupine's Quill 1992), and *For Whose Delight* (Mariscat 1995).

CATHERINE WALSH (b. 1964)
Born in Dublin, Walsh spent her childhood between there and rural Wexford. She left school at seventeen and took a variety of jobs before leaving to teach English in Barcelona with Billy Mills. With Mills she has run hardPressed poetry. They now live in Tallaght, near Dublin. Her books include *Short Stories* (North & South 1989), *Pitch* (Pig Press 1994), and *Idir Eatortha & Making Tents* (Invisible Books 1996).

BENJAMIN ZEPHANIAH (b. 1958)
Zephaniah was born in Birmingham, and his childhood was divided between England and Jamaica. After a period in approved school and prison (for burglary), he emerged as a defining voice of Rasta poetry in England, performing and recording extensively. His printed work includes *Pen Rhythm* (Page One Books 1981), *City Psalms* (Bloodaxe 1992), and *Propa Propaganda* (Bloodaxe 1996).

Acknowledgments continued from page iv

Roy Fisher for work from *The Cut Pages* (Fulcrum 1971, reprinted Oasis Shearsman 1986) and *Poems 1955–87* (Oxford University Press 1988).

Allardyce, Barnett, Publishers, for work from *Collected Poems and Translations* (Allardyce, Barnett 1990). Copyright © 1976, 1990 Jonathan Culler and the Estate of Veronica Forrest-Thomson. Copyright © 1990 Allardyce, Barnett, Publishers.

Ulli Freer for work first published in *Angel Exhaust* and unpublished work.

Harry Gilonis for work from *Reliefs* (HardPressed Poetry 1988, reprinted Pig Press 1990), *Shrike*, and *Formcards*.

Anthony Gormley and the Arts Council Collection, Hayward Gallery, London, for *Field for the British Isles*.

The Estate of Jonathan Griffin for work from *In Earthlight* (Menard Press 1995).

Bill Griffiths for work from *For Rediffusion* (New London Pride 1978), *Loot*, Amra Imprint, and *New American Writing*.

Alan Halsey for work from *Five Years Out* (Galloping Dog 1989) and *A Robin Hood Book* (West House 1996).

Lee Harwood for work from *Monster Masks* (Pig Press 1985) and *Morning Light* (Slow Dancer 1998).

Michael Haslam for work from *Continual Song* (Open Township 1986) reprinted in *A Whole Bauble* (Carcanet 1995).

Randolph Healy for work from *Envelopes* (Poetical Histories 1995) and *Rana Rana!* (Wild Honey Press 1997).

John James for work from *Striking the Pavilion of Zero* (Ian McKelvie 1975), *Berlin Return* (Grosseteste/Ferry/Delires 1983), and *Schlegel Eats a Bagel* (Equipage 1996).

Amryl Johnson and the London Arts Board for work first published in *London Arts Board News* (Autumn 1995).

Linton Kwesi Johnson and LKJ Music for work from *Tings an Times* (Bloodaxe/LKJ Music 1991).

Tom Leonard for work from *Etruscan Books Reader 5* (1998) and uncollected work.

Tony Lopez for work from *Stress Management* (Boldface Press 1994) and *False Memory* (The Figures 1996).

Rob MacKenzie for work from *Kirk Interiors* (Ankle Press 1994), *Off Ardglas* (Invisible Books 1997), and uncollected poems.

Barry MacSweeney for poems from *Farcliff Babylon* (Writer's Forum 1978), *Odes* (Trigram 1978), and *Pearl* (Equipage 1995).

Billy Mills for work first published in *Shearsman*.

Geraldine Monk for poems from *The Sway of Precious Demons* (North & South 1992) and uncollected work.

King's College London for work by Eric Mottram from *Selected Poems* (North & South 1989) and *Design Origins* (Amra 1994)

Wendy Mulford for *Nevrazumitelny* (Poetical Histories 1991).

Grace Nichols for poems from *Sunris* (Virago 1996). Reproduced with permission of Curtis Brown Ltd, London, on behalf of Grace Nichols. Copyright Grace Nicholas 1996.

Douglas Oliver for poems from *Kind* (Allardyce, Barnett 1987), *Three Variations on a Theme of Harm* (Paladin 1990), and *Penguin Modern Poets* 10 (1996).

Maggie O'Sullivan for work from *Unofficial Word* (Galloping Dog 1988) and *In The House Of The Shaman* (Reality Street 1993).

Tom Pickard for work from *Tiepin Eros* (Bloodaxe 1994).

Elaine Randell for work for *Songs for the Sleepless* (Pig Press 1982) and *Beyond All Other* (Pig Press 1986).

Tom Raworth for poems from *Tottering State* (The Figures 1984) and *Clean and Well Lit* (Roof Books 1996).

Carlyle Reedy for work originally published in *Slow Dancer*.

Denise Riley for poems from *Mop Mop Georgette* (Reality Street 1993).

The Estate of John Riley for poems from *Selected Poems* (Carcanet 1995).

Peter Riley for work from *Five New Poems* (Pig Press 1978), *Alstonefield* (Shearsman 1995), and uncollected work.

Maurice Scully for work from *Postlude* (Wild Honey Press 1997).

John Seed for poems from *History Labour Night* (Pig Press 1984), *Interior in the Open Air* (Reality Studios 1993), and uncollected work.

Gavin Selerie for poems from *Roxy* (West House Books 1996).

Robert Sheppard for sections from *Empty Diaries* (Stride 1998).

Colin Simms for poems from *Horcum and Other Gods* (Headland 1974), *Movement* (Pig Press 1980), *Shots at Otters* (RWC 1995), and uncollected work.

Iain Sinclair for poems from *The Ebbing of the Kraft*.

Chris Torrance for work from *Acrospirical Meanderings in a Tongue of the Time* (Albion Village 1973).

Gael Turnbull for work from *While Breath Persist* (Porcupine's Quill 1992) and *For Whose Delight* (Mariscat 1995).

Catherine Walsh for work from *Pitch* (Pig Press 1994) and *Idir Eatortha and Making Tents* (Invisible Books 1996).

Benjamin Zephaniah for work from *City Psalms* (Bloodaxe 1996), © Benjamin Zephaniah 1992.